Dedication

For my grandmothers,
Pearl F. Thomas and Mary Ellen Fraser.

HEALING
MIRACLES
for your
Family

**Practical Solutions for Helping Your
Loved One Experience a Healing Miracle**

Art Thomas

SUPERNATURAL TRUTH PRODUCTIONS, LLC
Practical Training for Spirit-Filled Living
www.SupernaturalTruth.com

Copyright © 2017, Art Thomas

TABLE OF CONTENTS

PREFACE

IN THE LAST FIVE YEARS, I HAVE ENJOYED THE
tremendous privilege of training tens of thousands of
Christians to minister healing to the sick in Jesus'
name. I've personally witnessed thousands of miracles
during this short period of time, most of them
happening through ordinary believers just like you.

Having a ministry that is noted for miracles
does, however, come with its hardships. Not
everyone to whom I minister is healed, and the
heartache of that is multiplied when the person not
healed is close family. It's not easy to travel halfway
around the planet to train Christians in the bush of
Africa when your own family and friends are sick
back home. How do you justify to your wife's family a
two-week trip to bring Jesus' healing and saving
power to another country when your wife's father is

at home battling cancer? They've never complained to me about this, but I'm sure they've thought of it if I have.

Healing ministry can be an emotional roller coaster. I have experienced the unique challenge of ministering healing to family—both with great success and with great disappointment. If I'm really honest with you, I know I don't have all the answers. All I can share with you in this book is what I have experienced and discovered thus far in my journey and hope that it will propel you further in your own walk with the Lord.

I regularly host question and answer sessions about healing ministry, and I preface each one with three promises:

1) If I don't know an answer, I will simply tell you, "I don't know."
2) If I have a guess or an unsubstantiated opinion, I will tell you that it is nothing more than that.
3) If I'm certain, I will tell you my answer with certainty; but that doesn't mean I'm right!

In other words, you're going to be responsible to take anything I say to the Bible and search to see whether or not it's true. The Bereans were called noble for testing Paul's words against the Scriptures. (See Acts 17:11.) Additionally, try putting my words into practice and see what the fruit is. As Jesus said, "Anyone who chooses to do the will of God will find out whether My teaching comes from God or whether I speak on My own." (See John 7:17.)

I should alert you up front that I am absolutely convinced that healing is always God's will. For some readers, that statement raises all sorts of red flags. Believe me, I was one of those readers as recently as 2008. But in 2009, I did a Biblical study of healing ministry that convinced me otherwise. It took a lot of critical thinking and scrutiny of the Scriptures to change my mind. I like to say that, until then, I had developed a very complicated theology to make me feel comfortable with my lack of results. I had all manner of questions and arguments from years of disappointments where healing is concerned, and I wasn't going to change my mind easily.

If that sounds like you, then this book is going to leave you with a lot of questions. I would recommend watching a few of the free videos on my YouTube channel (just search for my name and the word "healing"), reading some of the free articles on my web site about healing, or reading a copy of my book, *Spiritual Tweezers: Removing Paul's Thorn in the Flesh and Other False Objections to God's Will for Healing* (available at www.SupernaturalTruth.com).

But if you've already settled your conviction that God wants to heal, or if you're at least willing to suspend your questions for the sake of searching for some good advice, then this book should be an enjoyable read and a tremendous help to you.

As you read through these pages, I pray you

will be encouraged to minister healing to your family and that you will see results. I also pray that any emotional burden you've been carrying for your loved one will be surrendered to Jesus so that you can contend for their healing with freedom, faith, and rest.

Jesus wants your family to be healed even more than you do; He paid for it with His own blood. Trust Him in this partnership, and He will do all the heavy lifting.

Be blessed,

Art Thomas

INTRODUCTION

"DADDY, I HURT MY FOOT. WILL YOU PLEASE heal it?"

My five-year-old threw his leg unceremoniously across my lap as though it was a routine procedure. I gently grabbed hold of it and said, "Thanks, Jesus. How's that?"

"All better!" My boy skipped off to return to playing.

Jesus works better than kisses.

Welcome to my home life. Healing is normal here. It's expected. My two boys, Josiah and Jeremiah, are growing up in a house where miracles are seen on a regular basis and laying-hands is our first response to sickness.

And yet, we have also wrestled through long-term, chronic conditions that took years to

see resolved—some of them are still ongoing.
There is a bottle of Tylenol in our cupboard. I
hope you see that I'm not trying to falsely imply
that my house is some sort of utopia where
sickness disappears; but it is a place where
miracles happen and hope is the daily atmosphere.

It wasn't always this way. I remember
what it was like to hopelessly suffer with
degenerative disc disease. I remember being
convinced that my condition was God's will for
my life, looking forward to nothing more than a
possible future surgery. I remember what it was
like to "just deal with it."

I also remember what it was like to
struggle with that chronic pain after I came to
believe in God's will to heal me. I started
ministering healing in August of 2009. From then
until my healing in April of 2011, I watched God
heal other people's backs through my hands while
I was still needing serious pain medication to cope
with my own condition.

I remember the month before I was
healed. I was bedridden in excruciating pain. I
remember crying as my wife propped up my two-
month-old baby boy on my knees so that I could
feed him a bottle while lying in bed. I remember
thinking I would never be able to hold him or
wrestle with him or carry him on my shoulders.
Even though it was only a temporary bed-rest
until my bulging and degenerating discs relaxed

enough to walk safely, I questioned how I could possibly be planning to start a traveling ministry only a few weeks later. I could have never imagined grabbing my baby boy's foot only five years later and expecting an instant miracle—let alone seeing it happen.

But in April of 2011, at the tail end of my prescribed bed-rest and just days before my launch into traveling ministry, Jesus healed my back.

I also remember what it was like when three years into my traveling ministry, I started having intense stomach cramps and a serious bleeding problem (I had suffered mild cramping for my entire life but thought nothing of it). I put off going to the doctor for an entire year, hoping it would simply go away; but it only worsened. In the winter of 2015, I was diagnosed with Crohn's Disease. I continued watching other people receive healing from Jesus as He ministered through my hands, but many times I laid my hands on others while my own stomach was twisted in pain.

In July of 2015, Jesus healed me of Crohn's Disease. Today, as I write this over a year later, I can eat anything I want. (I'll share more about this experience in Chapter Ten.)

The insights I'm going to share in this book are things that my wife and I learned in the process of battling chronic, "incurable" conditions. I'm not interested in sharing a bunch of theories that don't actually help you. Instead, I want to give you practical tools and mindsets that will help you contend for your loved one's healing with faith, hope, and love. I can't guarantee a healing, but I can guarantee that Jesus has already done all the work necessary to accomplish the miracle.

I'm not here to teach you how to earn a miracle with a list of activities to perform. I'm here to teach you how to rest in faith while actively loving the family member who needs healing.

So relax. Jesus already did all the work.

Chapter 1

YOU CAN MINISTER HEALING
TO YOUR FAMILY

"I'M IN LABOR."

With my cell phone to my ear, I stood momentarily stunned as panic swept over me. My wife Robin was only twenty-four weeks pregnant with our second child, and the contractions were only about three minutes apart. This being our second child, Robin knew what active labor felt like, and this was it.

I left my shopping cart in the aisle at the grocery store and raced home. As I drove, the reality of what was happening began to set in. Tears poured from my eyes. I cried out loud to the Lord in desperation, "God, I can't! I can't do this! I'm not strong enough!"

Then came the gentle reply of Jesus deep within my spirit. It felt like my own thoughts, but I knew it was Him: *This is what it means when I say that My power is made perfect in your weakness.*

Peace overwhelmed the panic, and I suddenly knew everything would be okay. His grace was enough to get the job done.

I walked quickly into our house and calmly approached my wife who was leaning against the kitchen counter, having another contraction. I knelt down, laid my hands on her belly, and said in a gentle and peace-filled voice, "Contractions, stop now in Jesus' name."

Immediately, the contraction she was having stopped. I grabbed our overnight bag and helped my wife into the car. She had a few less-intense contractions in the car that were further and further apart. By the time we arrived at the hospital, they were finished, and the doctors couldn't find anything wrong at all.

Jeremiah James Thomas was born a little over ten weeks later—still a little early, but definitely in better condition than he would have been. And the miracles didn't stop there. We have medical documents declaring a "spontaneous closure" of a hole in his heart. Today as I write, our little boy is a healthy four-year-old who even ministers healing to others.

Some have suggested that it's harder to minister healing to our family members, but my experience is that this difficulty only exists between our own ears. We'll dig more into this issue in the next chapter, but for now I simply want to settle the idea that it's both possible and technically simple. You can minister healing to your family.

YOU CAN MINISTER HEALING

Jesus only gave one prerequisite for ministering healing: simple trust in Him.

> **John 14:12 –** Very truly I tell you, *whoever believes in Me* will do the works I have been doing, and they will do even greater things than these, because I am going to the Father. (*emphasis added*)

> **Mark 16:17-18 –** And these signs will accompany *those who believe:* In My name...they will place their hands on sick people, and they will get well. (*emphasis added*)

If you believe in Jesus, then you qualify. I have taught the principles of healing ministry all over the world. It doesn't matter if you live in an upper-class suburb in America, a crowded apartment complex in China, a village in the bush of Uganda, the slums of Haiti, the jungles of India, or the cinderblock buildings of Slovakia—the truth remains the same: Every believer in Jesus is authorized to heal in His name.

In five years of traveling the globe and training tens of thousands of people to minister healing (both in person and through video), I have personally witnessed around 4,000 miracles, most of which were performed through "ordinary Christians" as they ministered to each other in Jesus' name. If you've ever watched the ends of my sermons on YouTube, you've seen the testimonies as people report what God is doing through their fellow believers, one after the next. I've seen children minister healing who have been Christians for no longer than five minutes. I've seen elderly people minister healing who spent their lifetimes believing God couldn't possibly use them in that way. There are no limitations for those who place their faith in Jesus.

If you believe in Him, then you qualify.

How to Minister Healing

Before we can consider what it looks like to minister healing to family, it's a lot easier to start with what it looks like to minister healing to strangers.

Peter and John were walking to the Temple in Jerusalem at the normal time of prayer. As they approached the Gate Beautiful, they saw a crippled beggar who was being carried to the gate to beg for money. The beggar called out to Peter and John for some charity, but Peter responded with something better.

"I don't have any money," he said, "But let me give you what I do have. In the name of Jesus Christ of Nazareth, walk."

Peter grabbed the man's right hand, lifted him to his feet, and the crippled man was instantly and miraculously healed. (See Acts 3:1-10.)

There was no fancy prayer, no begging God, no pleading, no shouting (except from the healed man!), no preaching, no "atmosphere" music, no magic words—nothing.

When Peter and John were later questioned about the miracle, Peter identified the source of the man's healing: "It is Jesus' name and the faith that comes through Him that has made this man well, as you can plainly see." (See Acts 3:16.)

In Matthew 10:8 Jesus commanded His disciples to heal the sick. He never once said, "Ask My Father to heal the sick." Instead, He told them to do it. Some have suggested that this command was only for the Twelve Apostles, but remember the last command Jesus gave these same men: "Therefore go and make disciples of all nations...teaching them to obey everything I have commanded you..." (See Matthew 28:19-20.) In other words, if He commanded the Twelve to do it, then in most cases He commanded all of us to do it. Healing ministry is a command from Jesus for all who consider themselves His disciples.

Now, if that seems a little bit blasphemous to you, it's because there's a little bit of nuance needed. Jesus also said, "Apart from Me, you can do nothing." (See John 15:5.) When Jesus commanded His disciples to heal the sick, He knew they couldn't do it apart from Him, and He knows the same about us today. He also knew that they couldn't love their enemies apart from Him, fully love God apart from Him, or anything else apart from Him. Apart from Jesus, we can do nothing. Everything Jesus commands is an invitation to partner with Him. The command to heal, then, is an invitation to partner with Him in the ministry of healing.

I have preached and written extensively elsewhere about additional nuance in healing ministry. This book is less about the mechanics or theology of effective Christian healing ministry and more about applying that ministry in the context of your family. Given that, I'm going to offer you a simple "crash-course" here. What I'm sharing in this book is all you need to know to minister healing, but it probably isn't going to answer all of your questions. For that, I would point you to other materials.[1]

Healing ministry is actually very simple. Jesus told us how to do it in Mark 16:17-18. All we have to do is lay our hands on the person. He didn't even say that you're required to say anything (although you can).

In Luke 9:1, Jesus gave His disciples both power and authority to drive out demons and cure diseases. These two tools—power and authority—are the same tools available to us today.

Throughout the Gospels, we see God's power at work when the sick made physical contact with Jesus. (See Luke 6:18-19.) Sometimes physical contact isn't possible, but God also gives us authority to minister long-distance. Consider the Centurion who basically told Jesus, "I'm not worthy to have You set foot in my house. I'm a man under authority, and I have people under me, so whatever I command is done. I know that You are a man under authority, so simply say the word, and my servant will be made well." Jesus was amazed at his faith, spoke a word of authority, and the servant was healed long-distance. (See Matthew 8:5-13.)

At the temple gate, Peter used both tools. He spoke a word of command, telling the man to walk; and then he made physical contact with him, grabbing his right hand.

There's no formula and no method. But we do have two tools—power and authority—which are generally administered through physical contact and speech.

It's important to note that the phrase "in Jesus' name" isn't a string of magic words. It simply means, "I'm doing this on behalf of Jesus." As long as that concept is conveyed to the person, you've done what you're supposed to do. I know a man who often says, "Jesus heals you," and sees great results. I know another person who says, "On behalf of Jesus, I tell you…" and another who simply says, "As a representative of Jesus, I say…" Again, these are not magic words. I've seen plenty of cases where the name of Jesus wasn't spoken in that exact moment, but the person receiving ministry knew full well that what was happening was being done on Jesus' behalf. The concept itself is more important than what words are used.

While there is no method, there are tools (power and authority). And while there is no formula, there is a general pattern:

1. **Don't beg or ask God to heal the person.** Jesus told you to do it. So simply use one or both tools that are available to you: power and/or authority.

2. **Lay hands on the person if they'll let you.** There's no special formula for how. Some people were healed as they merely touched the edge of Jesus' robe with their fingertips. For others, Jesus touched the part of their body that was giving them the problem. Just make contact somehow if possible. If it's not possible or if the person doesn't want you to touch them, just move on to the next step.

3. **If you feel led, speak a word of command on behalf of Jesus.** This can be done with a smile on your face, with your eyes open, and with a gentle tone of voice. Your authority is not based on how loud or forceful you are. It is based on what Jesus has done to transform your life. (See Ephesians 2:4-7.)

4. **If the person is able to test their condition somehow, have them do so.** If they can't test it now, they can test it later—perhaps even with help from a doctor.

5. **If the person is healed, praise God! If not, minister healing again.** Continue with this pattern until the person is healed. (If the person cannot test things immediately, the

pattern is the same as if you can; it just takes longer.)

Allow me to simplify this further:

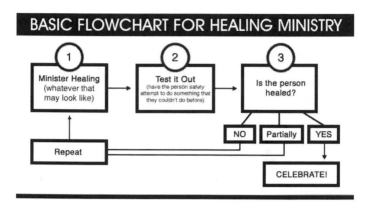

If a person's condition cannot be tested immediately, the pattern remains the same; it just takes longer.

There's more I'd love to add here, but that would derail us from our focus of ministering to family. Simply know this: There's always more to learn about healing ministry (I'm still learning too), but it all builds on this foundation: God wants it, Jesus paid for it, and all believers can do it; so put your hand on the person, speak in Jesus' name (if the Holy Spirit leads you—otherwise you don't have to say anything), and see what God does.

If we make it any more complicated than that, then we've missed the whole point of the Gospel. Everything is "by grace through faith." In other words, everything in the Christian life happens through the empowering and enabling favor of God (that's grace) as we actively trust the Holy Spirit to do His work (that's faith).

FAITH LIKE A CHILD

I like to say that faith is doing my part—and only my part—while completely trusting God to do the rest. The problem is that we often try to do some of God's part, or else we don't actually believe that He's going to come through unless we "try harder."

I was twenty-five years old the first time Jesus healed someone through my hands. Prior to that, I grew up in a church that believed in healing, and I even held credentials with a Pentecostal denomination for over a year. Yet throughout my entire life, healing ministry never seemed to work. The problem wasn't that I never tried. In fact, I prayed for hundreds of people to be healed without ever seeing results. During those first twenty-five years of my life, I begged God to heal, I bartered and made deals with God, I prayed very fancy prayers, I closed my eyes really tight and tried to somehow push power out my arm as I laid hands on the person. But the results never came. I never saw anyone healed that way.

By begging God, I proved that I didn't know His nature, assuming that I had more compassion than He did.

By bartering and making deals, I proved that I

didn't trust that the blood of Jesus was a sufficient motivation to convince God to heal (or, rather, evidence of His pre-existing will to heal).

By praying my fancy prayers, I proved that my faith was in my own eloquence instead of simply being in Jesus and the price He already paid for this person's healing.

And by squinting my eyes and trying to push power out my arm, I was proving that I didn't believe God would move unless I gave Him a shove.

I was trying to do part of His job for Him. I was trying to convince Him when He was already convinced.

But the most sobering realization I had was that all this time, I had been praying to the wrong god. The god I was seeking may have been the right one by name and association with Jesus, but his character was utterly different from the true God. I was approaching a god who was indifferent to human suffering, who cared less about the person in front of me than I did, who wouldn't hear my prayers unless I found the right combination of words to unlock his favor, and who didn't love me or the sick person enough to move unless I somehow performed to his standards.

That's the wrong god altogether; and if we're honest, that's the god many of us approach for healing.

When Jesus taught in Matthew 18:3 and Luke 18:17 that we need to be like little children in order to

enter the Kingdom of God, He was speaking as much
about our trust-level as He was talking about the
nature of our Father. God is faithful and trustworthy.
He is good, righteous, and loving. You don't need to
approach Him with caution. You don't have to
wonder if He's a safe caregiver. The reason we can
wholeheartedly trust Him is because He is
wholeheartedly trustworthy.

When you trust God like a child, it shows in
how you minister healing. Suddenly, you realize that
the only thing He told you to do was to lay hands on
the person. You've been authorized to speak in His
name (on His behalf), so you're allowed to do that
too.

Penny Mattos was at her daughter's house in
Texas. Her daughter kept telling her husband to have
his mother-in-law pray for him, but he kept brushing
it off. Finally, the daughter spoke up and said her
husband had a bad toothache. Penny knew her kids
couldn't afford the dental work. She figured her son-
in-law might not be comfortable with her laying
hands on him, so she just pointed at his mouth and
commanded his tooth to be healed. In her words,
"He got a funny look, rubbed his jaw, said it was
warm, and the pain was gone." And that pain never
returned. Penny found out later that her son-in-law
thought he needed to have faith also and didn't think
it would work for him. But when a child of God acts
in faith, anything is possible, and no one can stop it.
(Of course, now he believes!)

That's it. That's healing ministry. It really is simple. And when we trust our loving God in this childlike way, we start to see more results.

Do you remember the story I told at the beginning of this chapter about the birth of my youngest son, Jeremiah? When he was only two years old, my wife and he were playing in our living room with my oldest, Josiah. My wife, Robin, was sitting on the edge of the couch with her elbows on her knees when Josiah popped up beneath her and rammed his four-year-old head into her nose.

Everything went silent at the bone-chilling sound of a loud "crack." Blood instantly poured from Robin's nose.

Before I could make it there from across the room, Jeremiah toddled up to Robin and said, "You okay, Mommy?" Then he placed his hand on Robin and said, "Nose, be healed—Jesus' name."

Instantly, the bleeding stopped, the pain stopped, and there is still no sign whatsoever of a broken nose.

The lesson? Keep it simple. You can minister healing to your family.

ENDNOTES:

1 — Check out the "Additional Resources" page at the end of this book for a list of recommended materials that will give more detail about how to minister healing.

Chapter 2

UNDERSTANDING THE UNIQUE DIFFICULTY OF MINISTERING HEALING TO FAMILY

MY MOM AND DAD WERE BOTH SCHEDULED TO have cataract surgery on their eyes. I prayed for them. I spoke words of authority in Jesus' name over them. I did everything I knew to do, and both of them ended up having the surgery instead of a miracle.

Shortly after their surgeries, I ministered as an evangelist in Knoxville, Tennessee—about 40

minutes from where my parents live. My mom came
to the meeting and sat on the front row.

As the people of the little church ministered
to each other, many were healed. Then an old man
with a long, white beard and tattered overalls waddled
up to me.

"I've got one for ya," he said in a thick
southern accent, "Cataracts. I've got 20/200 vision in
this eye."

Great! I thought with an air of sarcasm,
Cataracts! I know this one...

As if to remind me of my previous
shortcoming, my mom was sitting right there on the
front row, just feet away from us. And she was seeing
the whole thing because she had surgery!

I realized that I was starting to psych myself
out, so I decided the best thing to do would be to
minister healing as quickly as possible. I didn't want
to give myself time to convince myself that it
wouldn't work!

"No problem," I answered the man. I quickly
placed my hand over his eye and said, "Cataracts, go
in Jesus' name." I pulled my hand back as quickly as I
had placed it there and asked, "How's that?"

What followed was the most animated
response that I have yet witnessed in healing ministry.
This elderly man's eyes opened wide with shock, and
he began whooping and shouting and jumping up and
down. Then, as if his engine had been revved up, he
took off running across the room and ran into the
wall at the other end, catching himself with his hands.

I'll be honest with you: This guy was such a
character that I wasn't sure whether he had been

healed or whether he was just a super-Pentecostal who felt a little "blessed."

"That's great!" I shouted to him, "But are you healed?"

The man spun around, looked again with wide eyes, and recommenced his frenzy of whooping, jumping, skipping, and running around the church.

"That's great!" I shouted again, "But can you see?"

It was as if I wasn't even in the room. Maybe I should have laid hands on his ears first.

Finally, the man sat down in a chair, out of breath from his wild dance, eyes darting all over the room.

"That's great," I said more calmly this time, "but can you see?"

"Yeah!" He answered, "I can see!"

Naturally, I had to process why it was so simple to minister healing to this old man—whose vision was worse than my parents' had been—and why I couldn't manage to find any shred of results when ministering to my own parents. The logical observer might conclude that it's just easier to minister to strangers than to family. And many healing ministers—in my experience—would tell you that's true.

IS THERE REALLY A DIFFERENCE?

Whenever I conduct healing meetings, I teach the church how to minister to each other in Jesus' name. Then I turn the people of the church loose on each other with one stipulation: "Don't go to your spouse." This isn't because you can't minister healing to your spouse, but experience has proven that I tend to see fewer results in meetings where spouses minister to each other. It's much easier to learn what faith is while ministering to someone with less emotional and relational strings attached. Then you can apply what you've learned in the context of your family.

Many healing ministers talk about the difficulty of ministering to family—I'm not alone in this. Many speculate as to why, but I would argue that the main issue is simply that we think it's more difficult. As you saw in Chapter One, ministry to family is possible. As I have said, most of the difficulty—if there is any—exists between our own ears.

I don't tell you this as someone who has completely conquered the struggle of ministering to family. Believe me, I'm in this battle right alongside you. Imagine what it's like for me to travel the world, witness scores of healings almost every weekend, and then come home to see my wife's grandmother who still doesn't have use of her right side after a head injury more than a year ago. Or my father-in-law who has had a double hip replacement and often struggles with back pain. Or my brother who has allergies and breathing issues. Or…

I think you get the point.

Add to that the unspoken pressure that is felt whenever I'm around family members who are skeptical of healing and wonder why—if what I say is true—I don't just heal all these people who are suffering in my own family.

Ministering healing to family isn't any more difficult than ministering healing to a stranger, but attempting to minister healing to family without results is definitely more difficult to navigate. We see those people on a regular basis and are faced with questions, discouragement, and sometimes even sarcastic comments from jaded loved ones who are tired of our "annoying optimism."[1]

Nevertheless, even if ministering healing to family is no more difficult than ministering to anyone else, why do many of us seem to see fewer results with family than we do with others? Why is it that I saw an old man in Knoxville healed of cataracts but not my own parents? Why is it that I've seen thousands of people receive restored mobility but not my wife's grandmother? Why is it that experience does not line up with truth?

I've spent considerable time meeting with the Lord about this issue, and I'll again be honest with you that I don't have all the answers. However, the Lord has shown me a few of my own shortcomings that need work, and I'll share them with you here in case it turns out to be beneficial in your own search for answers.

HOPE DEFERRED

Proverbs 13:12 says, "Hope deferred makes the heart sick, but a longing fulfilled is a tree of life." When you've been praying for something for a really long time without results, it's hard to snap out of discouragement and expect that "this is the time it's going to happen." In this way, we begin to put more faith in past experience than we do in Jesus.

When ministering to strangers, we have room to wonder later if the person was healed after we walked away, so that doesn't always haunt us the next time we minister to someone. When ministering to acquaintances, we don't have to see them constantly and be reminded that they are still sick. But when ministering to family, we cannot escape a lack of results. We see the person—in some cases, daily— and are usually directly impacted by that person's condition.

If we're not careful, a focus on the lack of results can make things even more difficult for us as our hearts become sickened with unbelief, doubt, fear, and discouragement. If you allow yourself to be a disciple of disappointment, you will reproduce disappointment. Instead, be a disciple of Jesus.

"But a longing fulfilled is a tree of life." In Scripture, the Tree of Life constantly bears fruit and is always able to nourish. (See Revelation 22:2.) Any longing that we have ever seen fulfilled has the power to nourish and sustain us through hardships if we will simply pick the fruit. In other words, remind yourself of the testimonies from the past. If you don't have any of your own, remember the testimonies of others. If you don't know any present testimonies, you at least have the testimonies of the Bible. (Appendix B of this book includes a number of testimonies from people who have walked with their family member through sickness until they saw a miracle.)

When ministering to loved ones, we need to nourish our faith by remembering and rehearsing the victories of the Lord in the past. Each time we minister, we should have the mindset that "this is the time it's going to happen." This is only possible when we take our attention off of how long our loved one has suffered and place it onto how long our God has been faithful.

MISAPPLIED COMPASSION

While there's nothing wrong with being moved with compassion for a person, I have experienced many situations where my feelings of compassion stood in the way of my faith. I became so deeply moved by a person's condition that I felt like "I need to take this one seriously." In doing so, I inadvertently implied that "this one won't be healed *unless* I take it seriously."

That's not faith in Jesus; it's faith in my seriousness. I believed that my intensity, passion, focus, or any other such merit would be the thing that will move God and bring the miracle.

But the real problem is not technically that I'm taking one condition more seriously than another. The real problem is that I'm taking most conditions less seriously than Jesus did when He went to the cross. Until I can learn to take headaches as seriously as Jesus took them (enough to suffer and die for people to be healed of them), I don't need to take cancer more seriously than headaches—both are the same. The problem is not that I'm taking cancer seriously (because no one takes it as seriously as Jesus); the problem is that I'm still seeing sickness through earthly compassion and not the heavenly compassion that drove Jesus to the cross for all of it.

Earthly compassion is based on the level of suffering being encountered, the severity of the condition, or the life-expectancy suggested by doctors. Heavenly compassion is based on the unfathomable love of God for all humanity that put His Son on the cross to pay the righteous price for everyone to be completely whole in body, soul, and spirit. Earthly compassion shrugs off minor aches and pains. Heavenly compassion goes to the cross for them.

If I'm honest with you, I'm still learning to let that reality sink in. It's hard for me to clearly see how to take "little things" as seriously as Jesus did. So until I can do that, I make my concern for minor issues the high-water-mark for how seriously I take "bigger things." If I'm casual about headaches, then I should be casual about cancer. The goal is to suspend my earthly compassion (which sees different conditions as being more or less serious) and start at the ground-level to grow in heavenly compassion (which sees all of it as an attack on the people for whom Jesus suffered and died). And I've learned that it works.

While ministering in China in 2016, I met a young man who had lesions on his brain stem that led to daily seizures, headaches, and blackouts (among other serious symptoms). As his mother explained what the doctors had said, I listened intently and found myself feeling true compassion for the teenager. I looked at them both with a smile and said, "Alright. Here's the deal. This is a serious condition for which Jesus paid a serious price. But I have learned that if I let this earthly reality get the best of me, I'll start putting effort into seeing you healed. My effort is not the source of your healing; Jesus' effort is. So I'm going to keep this very simple, place my hand on the back of your head, tell the brainstem to be healed, and that's it. Since you can't test it now, we'll just have to wait to see what happens."

That's exactly what I did. After my explanation, the actual time of ministry was less than 10 seconds. I did it with my eyes open, a smile on my face, and a voice that treated the condition as "no big deal" (because I recognized that Jesus has already done all the work). It didn't look particularly compassionate, nor did it seem like the appropriate expression of concern for the seriousness of the condition. But I knew that there was no sense begging God to heal the young man because I don't have more compassion than He does. I also knew that there was no sense trying to impress the people in the room. If this young man was going to be healed, it was going to be because of the power and love of Jesus and His shed blood, not because of my eloquence, seriousness, or performance.

Three days later the young man emailed me to say that for the first time in years, he had been symptom-free ever since that time of ministry. I received another report a month later that indicated the same.

When ministering to family, it's a lot harder to disconnect from the pressure to convey your love for the person through "taking things seriously" with earthly compassion. We want our loved ones to know that we care, and it feels crass to do things quickly or in a way that might look nonchalant. But the fact is that this is the posture of a heart that knows healing comes by grace through faith and not by works through performance, and it's the beginning of growing in heavenly compassion.

DEEP, EMOTIONAL INVESTMENT IN THE OUTCOME

Sometimes we place too much stock in the outcome of our healing ministry. In some cases, a lack of healing can shake our faith because we begin to believe things about God that aren't true. Other times, a lack of healing can devastate us because we treat each new ministry attempt as though it was our loved one's last chance at being set free.

If you're basing your theology of God's love and nature off of whether or not the healing happens, then your theology is misplaced. God's nature is not determined by miracles; miracles are determined by His nature. We must be so certain of who God is that natural circumstances don't shake us.

It's perfectly normal to "really hope this works" when you're ministering healing to someone you love. But that feeling of "I really hope this works" is sometimes just another form of saying, "This probably isn't going to happen." In this case, I'm putting more faith in the strength of the earthly situation (the problem) than I am putting faith in Jesus (the Solution).

As mentioned in the previous section, sometimes our compassion can get the best of us. We focus so much on our loved one's suffering that we struggle to see the simplicity of Christ's victory. Colossians 3:2 commands us, "Set your minds on things above, not on earthly things." Symptoms and suffering are earthly things. It is impossible to minister as we are supposed to when earthly things have our attention.

When ministering to family, keep your mind set on Jesus—His love, His victory, and His power to save. Rest in the fact that these are constants. If we don't see healing this time, it's not our loved one's last hope. Perseverance is biblical, and the Lord is still here with us in the midst of the trial.

JUDGING PEOPLE ON THEIR MERIT

When you know a person, you're often well aware of the lifestyle choices that brought on their condition.

If I'm on the street or in a church service and a stranger says, "I have diabetes," I think, *No problem.* In contrast, when someone whose unhealthy lifestyle I personally know says, "I have diabetes," I might think, *Of course you do. Now lay off the Twinkies!*

What I'm inadvertently saying is that God won't heal this person because they don't deserve it—as though the grace of God was something to be earned anyway. I'm putting more faith in the person's lifestyle choices than I am putting faith in Jesus. The whole point of the cross is that Jesus' sacrifice is more powerful than the worst decisions of mankind.

All over the world, I meet people after healing meetings who still have their condition and say, "I feel like I just don't deserve to be healed."

My answer? "You're right. You don't deserve healing. Nobody does. The only thing any of us deserves is death!" (See Romans 6:23.) This isn't about what the person deserves; it's about what Jesus deserves. Then I lay hands on them, and many times they're healed!

On the other side of the coin, sometimes we celebrate the merit of the person. We think things like, *This person has served God so faithfully for so many years—of course He will heal them.* But this too is faith in the person's merit rather than the work of Jesus on their behalf.

Healing never happens because we deserve it. Healing happens because Jesus deserves it. If my motivation is the merit of the person, then I have missed the heart of God, and I'm not truly trusting Him.

When ministering to family, look past the lifestyle choices, sinful decisions, and mistakes they've made. Look past the person's faithfulness and good deeds. Offer the hope of victory through Jesus. I'm not saying that we should ignore an unhealthy lifestyle, but I am saying that we should not base our expectation of that person's healing on their behavior. While overall health can be earned through self-discipline and wise habits, healing is not something that can be earned. Sometimes a healing is just the spark needed to motivate someone to start taking care of his or her body in a healthier way.

FEAR

It's not uncommon for us to have a greater sense of fear when ministering to family than when ministering to others. That fear is usually rooted in "what if" statements; and chief among them is, "What if this doesn't work?"

All the possible scenarios run through our mind. Perhaps our fear of it not working is more based upon our fear of rejection or failure. Perhaps our fear of it not working is more based upon a fear of what will happen to the person we love so much. Regardless of the motivating principle behind our fear, the reality beneath the surface is a lack of trust in the goodness of God.

When we can see the goodness of God, not only is it easier to trust that He will come through and bring the healing we seek, but we also trust Him to work things out in righteousness, kindness, and compassion even if the healing doesn't happen. Fear assumes the worst about God's character. Faith rests in the peace of knowing His love. First John 4:18 says that "perfect love drives out fear."

When ministering to family, don't worry about the "what ifs." Simply trust the goodness and love of God that transcend miraculous intervention. He will continue to be near to us and our loved ones, no matter what.

ENDNOTES:

1 — There is a temptation here to chalk things up to "the will of God," but our best understanding of God's will is seen in the life and ministry of Jesus, and He healed all. Besides that, the issue of God's will wouldn't answer why so many healing ministers see greater results outside their own family. Surely God didn't single out the families of healing ministers to suffer more than others. The most sensible answer—no matter how uncomfortable it may be—is that the weakness lies within us as ministers.

Chapter 3

You Don't Have to Carry This Burden Alone— Taking the Pressure Off

There's only one situation in the New Testament when a follower of Jesus tried to minister healing in Jesus' name without results.

Jesus, Peter, James, and John were up on a mountain, and the other nine disciples were down in the valley. A man brought his deaf and mute son to the remaining nine and told them a heartbreaking story about how an evil spirit had tried multiple times to kill his son by giving him seizures that would hurl him into water or fire. The disciples made an attempt at healing the boy in Jesus' name, but no matter how many results they had seen in the past, they couldn't seem to bring the boy to freedom.

By the time Jesus, Peter, James, and John came down the mountain and approached the group, the nine disciples and the teachers of the law were embroiled in an intense argument amid a crowd of spectators. Whenever we have a lack of results, we like to produce arguments. We like to come up with reasons why it didn't happen. We like to place blame. *Maybe the little boy didn't have enough faith. Maybe the boy's father didn't have enough faith. Maybe the crowd of onlookers didn't have enough faith. Maybe God wants the boy to have this condition. Maybe it's for some higher purpose, to bring God glory. Maybe God wants to heal him, but it just isn't the right time...*

We say these things, but Jesus never said these things. And if we're really honest, the only reason we say these things is because we don't believe Jesus actually revealed God's will when He healed all—and the excuses make us more comfortable in the face of our own lack of results.

When Jesus learned about the boy's condition, He said, "Bring the boy to Me." Jesus commanded the spirit to leave the boy and never return. Instantly, the boy was set free and healed.

Jesus disproved all the arguments. He made

no excuses. Instead, He brought victory where the disciples had not.

Later, the disciples asked why it was that Jesus could do what they could not. Just as important as His answer is what He didn't answer. Jesus did not say that it was because He's God and they're mere humans. Although technically true, this was not the issue that made the difference. He also didn't say that it wasn't God's will to heal the boy until He came on the scene. All the other possible arguments were proven false by the fact that Jesus succeeded where the disciples had not—this wasn't a problem with the boy's faith, the father's faith, the crowd's faith, or anything else like that. It worked for Jesus.

Before we look at Jesus' answer, I want to make sure you see this: Jesus didn't blame the boy or the boy's father for the lack of results.

FAMILY IS OFF THE HOOK

Even though the boy's father confessed his own unbelief in Mark 9:24, Jesus didn't identify that as the problem the disciples were having. He didn't say, "You should have helped the boy's father believe, and then it would have worked."

Jesus understands the unique difficulty of ministering healing to family. He understands all the challenges discussed in the previous chapter that make it difficult to simply trust God when someone you love is suffering. And the great news that we can

45

infer from this story is that Jesus does not hold family members responsible when their loved ones aren't healed.

If you're a parent or family member seeking healing for a child or loved one, the pressure is off. Jesus understands what you're facing, and as you'll see more clearly in the next chapter, He's proud of you for all you're doing.

Biblically speaking, the only role we see parents playing in the physical healing of their children is bringing the children to Jesus. None of them were expected to have the faith to heal the child themselves. The only faith expected of them was faith that someone else could bring the healing that was needed.

When the Canaanite woman came to Jesus to plead for her daughter's healing in Matthew 15:21-28, she called Jesus "Lord, Son of David." This woman recognized that Jesus was the Messiah—a name that means "anointed one." But that doesn't mean that she knew Jesus was God in the flesh. Most (if not all) people at the time were unaware of Jesus' divinity. So whenever Jesus marveled at someone's faith or said, "Your faith has healed you," He wasn't talking about their perfect faith in God. If it was their perfect faith in God that brought the healing, then the person could have been healed on their own without coming to Jesus (remember, they didn't know that He was God).

Like the Canaanite woman, some recognized

Jesus as the Anointed One (at best). Others called Him a prophet. Many just called Him "rabbi" or "teacher." Since we know the full story and therefore know about Jesus' divinity, it's hard to comprehend what it must have been like for the people who came to Jesus then. But if you put yourself in their position, Jesus was (as far as they knew) nothing more than a human being who consistently ministered God's miraculous power to heal. So when Jesus commented on someone's faith, He was actually identifying their faith in Him as a healing minister.

In the case of the Canaanite woman, she begged Jesus to heal her daughter and refused to stop seeking Him for the miracle. Finally, Jesus marveled at her faith and healed the girl long-distance. Remember, in the woman's mind, she wasn't pleading with God or chasing after God; she was pleading with the "anointed one"—the "Christ" who carried the promised Holy Spirit. Peter described Him saying, "...how God anointed Jesus of Nazareth with the Holy Spirit and power, and how He went around doing good and healing all who were under the power of the devil, because God was with Him." (See Acts 10:38.) And this description is true of many believers as well—anointed with the Holy Spirit and power, partnered with the ever-present God.

FINDING "ANOINTED ONES"

As family of your sick loved one, either you're

a Spirit-empowered believer or you're not. If you're
not, then you need to be. I highly recommend you
look into what it means to be baptized in the Holy
Spirit, clothed with God's power as Jesus promised.
(See Luke 24:49, Acts 1:4-8, and 2:1-4.) But if you are,
then you may very well be the one God uses to
minister healing to your family member. (I should
note that it *is* possible to minister healing without
being empowered through Spirit Baptism because
even those who haven't been baptized in the Holy
Spirit still have authority as believers in Christ. If you
don't yet have power, you can still use authority.)

With that said, remember all that we have
discussed so far. God understands our limitations in
ministering to family, and He doesn't hold that
against us. If you don't have faith for the person's
healing, at least have faith in the people He has
anointed in the earth to minister effectively. I'm not
saying that you need to hunt down big-name
preachers and faith-healers. Remember, even children
can minister healing. All you need to do is find
another believer who knows and loves Jesus. Find
anyone who has the Holy Spirit. "We" are the body
of Christ, and everyone who touched Jesus' body
when He walked this earth was healed.

Paul addressed this with the Corinthian
church. He pointed out their many divisions and the
fact that the rich were excluding the poor at their
feasts. (See 1 Corinthians 11:17-34.) Then he said that
the people were failing to discern the Lord's body and

were therefore eating and drinking judgment upon themselves. "That is why many among you are weak and sick, and a number of you have [died]. But if we were more discerning with regard to ourselves, we would not come under such judgment." (See 1 Corinthians 11:29-30.)

I used to think this verse was saying that when I partake in the bread and cup of communion, I have to somehow discern Jesus' body in the bread. But the context—emphasized throughout the following chapters—is that we are all His body, and we need to discern that we are all therefore equal. If more people would recognize that we are all extensions of Jesus' body on the earth, then there would be fewer sick and dying people among us. Why? Because we would actually go to each other for healing ministry instead of waiting for a celebrity preacher to show up and lay hands on us.

There's nothing in the Bible prohibiting sick Christians from laying hands on themselves or ministering to their own bodies in Jesus' name. There's nothing in the Bible prohibiting the Christian family of a sick person from ministering to them in Jesus' name. Both are allowed, and both have been known to bear fruit. But the only biblical prescription for a sick Christian is to go to other mature believers in their own church for ministry. (See James 5:14-15.)

So if the sick person ministers to himself and has success, great! If not, there's no pressure because the Bible doesn't make it his responsibility. Likewise, if you minister to your family member or loved one with success, great! If not, there's no pressure because the Bible doesn't make it your responsibility either.

Again: The pressure is off.

When the nine disciples in the valley couldn't bring healing to the epileptic boy, they asked Jesus why. Again, the boy and his father were left out of the equation. They had nothing to do with the lack of healing. They were already doing the only things expected of them simply by being present and seeking ministry. Instead, Jesus looked at the disciples (collectively) and said, "Because *you* have so little faith. Truly I tell you, if you have faith as small as a mustard seed, you can say to this mountain, 'Move from here to there,' and it will move. Nothing will be impossible for you." (See Matthew 17:20, emphasis added.)

The responsibility for faith falls on the Body of Christ collectively. We are representatives of Jesus. We are His disciples—all of us. Your sick loved one is not your responsibility alone. You're part of a family of "anointed ones" who are commissioned by Jesus to represent Him in unity with each other and with Him.

WE'RE ALL IN THIS TOGETHER

When you get right down to it, the shortcomings described in Chapter Two are logical weaknesses. The more deeply we care about someone, the more difficult it is to rest in faith. God understands these weaknesses, and that's why He doesn't make us responsible to minister healing to our family members. Are we allowed to? Absolutely. But should we feel bad if it doesn't work? Not at all.

Romans 15:1 tells us, "We who are strong ought to bear with the failings of the weak and not to please ourselves." Similarly, Galatians 6:2 commands us, "Carry each other's burdens, and in this way you will fulfill the law of Christ." Your healing or your loved one's healing is the responsibility of the rest of the Body of Christ. Those who aren't affected by the emotional battle of sick family are supposed to rally around you and help you and your loved one find victory through Jesus. The responsibility for faith is on the rest of us as ministers—not on your sick family member and not on you as their relative.

If your church isn't flocking to you, remember that the sick person's responsibility in James 5 is to seek out ministry from other believers. And if your sick family member is not going, then the biblical example is that you—as that person's family—can seek out healing on their behalf. You don't even have to bring that person with you (as proven by the Centurion and by the Canaanite woman).

Let me simplify this for you: Scripture never places the weight of responsibility for someone's healing on their family. Scripture never places the weight of responsibility on the sick person (with the exception of encouraging them to proactively seek out ministry from others). The responsibility only falls to those in the Body of Christ who are not weakened by the emotional struggle of watching a loved one suffer. (It's good to note here that there's a difference between taking responsibility and carrying the emotional burden of people not being healed. We are to cast our emotional burdens on Jesus and not carry them ourselves. See Psalm 55:22 and 1 Peter 5:7.)

You're allowed to minister healing to family, but God understands our weaknesses and has made a way for us.

I share all this to help take any unbiblical pressure off of your shoulders and help you to see that you're not alone in this journey. You're part of a family of anointed ones who are responsible to help fight alongside you with simple faith and genuine love.

With that groundwork laid, I'm going to use the rest of this book to teach you how to grow in your effectiveness in healing ministry and fulfill your role in ministering to your sick family (a role that is bigger than merely ministering healing). Some of my advice will be so practical that it almost seems unspiritual, and some of it will help you renew your mind so that you can expect miracles and even see them happen. As you read, remember that there's no pressure on you. But be encouraged that, as discussed in Chapter One, you can indeed minister healing to your family.

THE HIGH CALLING OF
CARING FOR THE SICK

I WAS INVITED TO SPEAK AT A SMALL CHURCH IN
Kentucky. The pastor and his wife, Jack and Geri
Stanley, had a twenty-one-year-old daughter named
Gentry who weighed forty-six pounds. They had been
believing for a miracle for nineteen years.

Gentry had been a healthy baby girl until
suffering a brain injury from baby vaccines at six
months old. Since then, she required twenty-four-
hour care, and the Stanleys rarely slept more than four

hours at a time. Geri said it was like having a newborn baby for the last twenty years.

When I came to the family's home, my heart broke for all of them. They had an entire room full of medical apparatus, including a hospital bed, feeding pumps, oxygen tanks, and a specialized wheelchair. In the corner was an extremely worn rocking recliner where Jack and Geri have spent hundreds of hours rocking their daughter—sometimes all night.

When you're a healing minister who has seen as many miracles as I have, the only thing you can think about in a situation like this is wanting to see that young woman's body uncurl and climb out of bed. You know what is possible, and you know it's God's will. You know that if Jesus were standing there in the room, that young woman would instantly receive strength and begin dancing around the room in praise to God.

But I'm still learning to be like Jesus, and I didn't see the results He would have seen.

In healing ministry, it can be easy to become distracted with wanting to look like Jesus and miss an opportunity to minister to Jesus.

MINISTERING TO JESUS

In Matthew 25, Jesus taught about the final judgment. Read this carefully, and see if you can identify where Jesus was in the room when I met with that family:

Matthew 25:31-46 – [Jesus said,] "When the Son of Man comes in His glory, and all the angels with Him, He will sit on His glorious throne. All the nations will be gathered before Him, and He will separate the people one from another as a shepherd separates the sheep from the goats. He will put the sheep on His right and the goats on His left.

"Then the King will say to those on His right, 'Come, you who are blessed by My Father; take your inheritance, the kingdom prepared for you since the creation of the world. For I was hungry and you gave Me something to eat, I was thirsty and you gave Me something to drink, I was a stranger and you invited Me in, I needed clothes and you clothed Me, I was sick and you looked after Me, I was in prison and you came to visit Me.'

"Then the righteous will answer Him, 'Lord, when did we see You hungry and feed You, or thirsty and give You something to drink? When did we see You a stranger and invite You in, or needing clothes and clothe You? When did we see You sick or in prison and go to visit You?'

"The King will reply, 'Truly I tell you, whatever you did for one of the least of these brothers and sisters of Mine, you did for Me.'

"Then He will say to those on His left, 'Depart from Me, you who are cursed, into the eternal fire prepared for the devil and his angels. For I was hungry and you gave Me nothing to eat, I was thirsty and you gave Me nothing to drink, I was a stranger and you did not invite Me in, I needed clothes and you did not clothe Me, I was sick and in prison and you did not look after Me.'

"They also will answer, 'Lord, when did we see You hungry or thirsty or a stranger or needing clothes or sick or in prison, and did not help You?'

"He will reply, 'Truly I tell you, whatever you did not do for one of the least of these, you did not do for Me.'

"Then they will go away to eternal punishment, but the righteous to eternal life."

When I stood in the Stanley's home with all the medical equipment, where was Jesus in the room? Yes, I know He's everywhere, and I know that we were all members of Christ's body. But sometimes it's easy to see Jesus everywhere except in the sick person. When Jesus spoke about the final judgment, even the righteous didn't realize that Jesus was present in the sick people to whom they ministered.

When you have a sick family member, it's easy to look at them in their suffering and question, "Where are You, Jesus?"

He's right there.

Look past the suffering, the agony, and the sickness, and look into the eyes of your loved one. Jesus is there, suffering right along with them—fully aware of everything they're enduring.

Jesus is able to empathize with our weaknesses. (See Hebrews 4:15). Isaiah 53:3 says of Jesus, "He was despised and rejected by mankind, a man of suffering, and familiar with pain. Like one from whom people hide their faces He was despised, and we held Him in low esteem."

Jesus bore your loved one's suffering on the cross. When you see suffering, you see Jesus.

LOVE IS TOP PRIORITY

Whenever I read the above passage from Matthew 25, I am struck by the fact that Jesus didn't say, "I was sick and you healed Me." He said, "I was sick and you looked after Me."

When we stand before Jesus at the final judgment, we're not going to have to answer for whether or not we ever successfully healed the sick in His name, but we are going to have to answer for whether or not we loved. In fact, it's the people who point to their success in working miracles to whom Jesus responds, "I never knew you. Away from Me, you evildoers!" (See Matthew 7:21-23.)

Paul wrote, "...if I have a faith that can move mountains, but do not have love, I am nothing." (See 1 Corinthians 13:2.) A few verses later, he states, "Love never fails." (See 1 Corinthians 13:8). In Paul's mind, if the miracle works but I don't love, then I've failed. On the other hand, if the miracle doesn't happen and yet I successfully loved, then I didn't fail. Love never fails.

Notice that Paul didn't say the *miracle* was nothing but rather, "*I* am nothing." When we minister without love, we offer only empty shells—God's image being only skin-deep. While the *activity* of God is seen, the *substance* of God is absent because "God is love." (See 1 John 4:8.) We were created in God's image—not merely as an external reality but in the sense that the fullness of who we are is designed to look like the fullness of who He is. You were created to embody love.

The fullest revelation of Jesus happens when "Christ the Victor" and "Christ the Suffering Servant" are seen together. Both are opposite ends of the spectrum of who Jesus is, but both are Jesus. And whenever a believer who is walking in the victory of Christ loves someone who is experiencing suffering, Jesus is revealed in ways that could not happen any other way.

Ideally, this situation results in a miracle; but Jesus is less impressed with miraculous results than He is impressed with love. For the sake of the person, we want a miracle; for the sake of Jesus, we want love; for the sake of all, we want both—and so does Jesus.

CARING WHILE MINISTERING

I have witnessed some of the most bone-headed actions and words coming from people who are more focused on healing than they are on love. Some of the worst come from denying the sick practical care and comfort while they are not yet experiencing their healing. Other times, we heap condemnation on the sick, blaming them for the condition they're in rather than taking responsibility ourselves as ministers.[1]

But the example we see in Scripture is something different. In James 5:14-15, we read, "Is anyone among you sick? Let them call the elders of the church to pray over them and anoint them with oil in the name of the Lord. And the prayer offered in faith will make the sick person well; the Lord will raise them up. If they have sinned, they will be forgiven."

I grew up in a Pentecostal church. Our pastor always had a bottle of anointing oil behind the pulpit. When people were sick, they could come to the front after the church service; and the pastor, the deacons, and the elders would lay hands on them while the pastor dabbed his finger in the oil and ceremonially smeared it on the person's forehead. Now there's nothing wrong at all with this practice (unless we treat the oil like a sort of Pentecostal magic potion), but it's probably not what James had in mind when he wrote his letter.

The Jewish New Testament Commentary says of this scripture:

> Anointing with oil is not merely a ceremony. In biblical times, olive oil was medicine (Isaiah 1:6, Lk 10:34), and being anointed with oil was considered physically pleasant (Psalms 23:5, 133:2-3).[2]

Furthermore, When Jesus gave instructions about those who are fasting, He instructed the disciples to "put oil on your heads...so that it will not be obvious to others that you are fasting..." (See Matthew 6:17-18.) In this sense, its use was cosmetic.

The fact is, you don't need a commentary to tell you that "anointing with oil" was a medicinal practice in those days (the word "anoint" sounds somehow sacramental but simply means "to smear"). Look no further than Jesus' parable of the Good Samaritan in which the Samaritan man went to the victim of a violent mugging and "bandaged his wounds, pouring on oil and wine." (See Luke 10:34.) The oil was used to soothe and disinfect.

It is very likely, therefore, that James' instruction to anoint with oil was less about a ceremonial ritual and more about caring for the sick person while you minister.

In today's world, that means letting people take whatever medications they've been prescribed by medical professionals, ministering with gentleness and compassion, and simply being considerate.

Famed Bible teacher Dr. J. Vernon McGee doesn't often side with Pentecostals and Charismatics in his interpretation of Scripture, but I appreciate his treatment of this passage:

> There are two Greek words which are translated "anoint" in the New Testament. One of them is used in a religious sense; that word is *chriō* in the Greek. From that we get the word *Christos*; Christ was the Anointed One. It means to anoint with some scented unguent or oil. It is used only five times in the New Testament, and it refers to the anointing of Christ by God the Father with the Holy Spirit.
>
> That second word translated "anoint" is *aleiphō*. It is used a number of times in the New Testament. . . Trench comments that *aleiphō* is "the mundane and profane word." The other, *chriō*, is "the sacred and religious word." The word used in this verse in James is *aleiphō,* and all it means is to rub with oil. You remember that when Hezekiah was sick, they put something medicinal on that boil he had. James is saying something very practical here. He says, "Call for the elders to pray, and

go to the best doctor you can get." You
are to use medicine, my friend. It is a
mistaken idea to say that this refers to
some religious ceremony of putting a
little oil from a bottle on someone's
head, as if that would have some
healing merit in it. It has no merit
whatsoever. James is too practical for
that.[3]

No medication is more powerful than Jesus,
so don't let yourself slip into the trap of thinking that
God can't heal a person unless they quit their
medicine. I have seen far too many people healed
while still receiving medical treatment. My own back
was healed while I was still taking prescription-
strength opioids for my pain.

It is impossible to qualify yourself for a
healing, and it is therefore also impossible to
disqualify yourself.

One month after Jeremiah Hembree's son
was born, his wife, Heather, suffered three strokes,
leaving her largely unresponsive. Doctors said she
wouldn't make it through the night. The first night,
Jeremiah fought through all the "why" questions and
struggled to imagine how he would raise their baby on
his own. But after three days of Heather being largely
non-communicative, she made almost a complete
turnaround—though she was mostly paralyzed on
one side and had very limited communication ability.
The doctors gave little hope of any further recovery,

but Jeremiah and others continued to pray for a miracle while Heather continued attending physical therapy. In a couple months she was able to walk unaided, and today you would never know she'd ever had a stroke—let alone three!

Heather's medical care didn't disqualify her from being healed, and neither did Jeremiah's wrestling with his faith. He said, "The long haul was a challenge. There were days I really hoped and believed for a total miracle, and honestly, there were days of total frustration and anger as to why God wasn't moving faster." But he prayed for her healing daily and took every opportunity he could for others to minister as well. Jeremiah's advice is, "Hold steady! Whether instantaneous or progressive, God is faithful and still in the healing business."

Medical care often prolongs length-of-life and/or quality-of-life while the rest of the Church grows into the faith necessary to bring the miracle Jesus purchased.

I want to be careful with this next example because there is no such thing as a "faith-o-meter" that must be filled up before we can see miracles; but imagine a person is told that they have two years to live unless they receive a medical treatment that will likely extend their life to five years. Now imagine it will take the Church four years to mature into the image of Christ in this particular area and successfully minister the miracle. What should the person do? I would suggest that the medication is probably a good idea. And in the mean time—until the Church matures in that area—our role is to love extravagantly.

THE ONLY THING THAT MATTERS

Again, when we stand before Jesus, the one question on His mind will be whether or not we loved. I should be clear that I'm not talking about being justified by works (earning our way into eternal peace through good deeds or earthly activity). We can only be saved by the work of Jesus. If we think that any work of our own will grant us access to God's eternal Kingdom, then we do not understand the Gospel. God's mercy and grace are freely available and can only be accessed by those who completely trust in the complete sufficiency of Jesus' work.

However, the New Testament has more than enough teaching about heavenly rewards and positions in the Kingdom that are indeed based on our works here on earth. Your salvation hinges only on the work of Jesus and whether or not you have put all your faith in Him to save you completely. But your eternal reward will be proportionate to your faithfulness to serve Him in partnership with the Holy Spirit.

In some ways, I have an easy job. As a traveling minister, I can swoop into a place like the Stanleys' home in Kentucky, give it my best shot, and then travel back home to be with my family. I'm responsible to love that sick person for the brief time I'm there, but at some point—and I hate to say it—I'm sort of "off the hook." If the healing doesn't happen, I can go back to my comfortable home, but that family is still in their heartbreaking situation of caring for their sick loved one.

When they and I stand before Jesus, they will likely have the greater reward.

I don't say that lightly. Granted, I know there are other factors, but I want to be clear that the mandate to love in Jesus' name is far greater than the mandate to heal in Jesus' name. Those who care for sick family members are doing something of eternal value. We all have roles to play as we contend in simple faith for the miracles Jesus made possible.

People like Jack and Geri Stanley are heroes to me. If I were to find myself in a similar situation, I can only pray that I would have the same faith and fortitude to stand firm, contending for a miracle, while simultaneously loving and caring so deeply and faithfully no matter how long it takes.

It's hard to teach simple faith for miracles and simultaneously teach how to function when the miracle hasn't yet come. I never want to plant ideas in people that cause them to expect miracles to take a long time. In Jesus' ministry, the answer was always, "Now is the day of salvation." (See 2 Corinthians 6:2.) Every time you minister healing, you should expect this to be the time the instant miracle will happen. But if it doesn't, the good news is that you have more time to love Jesus in a way that you will never be able to love Him on the other side of this life. In eternity, there will be no sick people. Love Jesus by loving the sick while you still can.

You will be thanked by Jesus for what you did as you faithfully loved and cared for your sick family member. Your actions matter to His heart. Whatever you do for that person, you are doing for Jesus. Contend for the miracle because Jesus deserves to receive everything for which He paid. But if it hasn't yet happened, celebrate the privilege of loving Jesus through practical, hands-on care for the sick.

ENDNOTES:

1 — I'd like to note here that if the sick person *must* be any part of the equation for their healing to happen, then Jesus could not have ministered with 100% results; yet He did. If you're asking, "What about the time Jesus couldn't work many miracles in His hometown?" check out my article at http://supernaturaltruth.com/why-couldnt-jesus-heal-in-his-hometown/

2 — Stern, David H. Jewish New Testament Commentary, Jewish New Testament Publications, Clarksville, MD, 1992, p. 741.

3 — Taken from *Thru the Bible, V,* by J. Vernon McGee, Copyright © 1983 by J. Vernon McGee. Used by permission of Thomas Nelson. www.thomasnelson.com

Chapter 5

HOW MUCH IS TOO MUCH?

A HUSBAND AND WIFE SAT IN FRONT OF ME, holding hands. Both had severe health problems and wanted to know how to pursue the miracles they knew Jesus wanted.

Earlier that night I preached about healing ministry and led several people into the first step of deciding to follow Jesus, and then the people of the church ministered healing to each other. Lots of miracles happened that night. A woman's deaf ear opened up, a man's arthritis pain left, another woman walked away from her crutches, and more. An entire

Hindu family (six adults and some children) came to salvation. It was an awesome night! But here sat this couple on the front row, holding hands and wondering why they hadn't yet been healed.

Three or four people had laid hands on them, including me; but the breakthrough didn't come.

I like to take time with people when I minister to them. Whenever possible, I like to give next-steps that will help people to grow in their faith and hope. I said to this couple, "If Jesus had been standing here, you two would be jumping up and down and running circles around this room right now. Instead, you got me; and I'm still learning to be like Him. The good news is, both of you just learned how to minister healing, and you can persevere for this for each other."

That's when I received one of the first questions that ever made me think critically about the unique challenges of ministering to family: "How often should we minister healing to each other?"

It's such a simple question, but it comes with so much baggage. My first response was that we have to be careful with that line of thinking because it implies that we don't expect God to do something immediately. I admonished them, "You have to go into this expecting that your miracles can still happen tonight. Every time you minister to each other, you need to come with the mindset that 'the most likely time for a miracle to happen is *right now* because *right now* is the moment I'm ministering.' If you think the miracle is going to happen tomorrow, then what's the point of ministering today? Try to fight the temptation to think long-term when it comes to miracles. Now, with that said, let's talk about a contingency plan…"

I realized that the struggle behind this couple's question was realistic and needed practical solutions. Behind their simple question were deeper, more specific questions: *If this takes a long time, how many hours a day are we supposed to lay hands on each other? If the miracle doesn't happen, how do we stop ministering and carry on with our day? More than that, how frequently should we be ministering to each other? Should we say, "Be healed!" every time we pass each other in the house? Should we deviate from our normal lives to just sit around and lay hands on each other all day?*

As I spoke to this couple, the Holy Spirit gave me a "word of wisdom"—a spiritual gift through which a person becomes aware of a nugget of Jesus' wisdom and speaks it out. I had never considered this answer until that moment when it poured out of my mouth. I'll share it with you in a moment, but first, I want to lay some groundwork.

HOW TO PURSUE A MIRACLE

Before we can effectively talk about matters of frequency in healing ministry, we have to start with a basic understanding of what it looks like to pursue a miracle long-term.

Again, I want you to be careful that you don't let this information cause you to expect things to take a long time. This teaching is only the backup plan.

There are five basic principles to pursuing a miracle:

(1) Remember testimonies. If you have personal testimonies of healing, remind yourself of these things. If not, study the testimonies of others. Read the miracle stories in Scripture. Let God renew your mind to expect His miraculous intervention in the earth.

(2) Remind yourself that "Now is the day of salvation." (See 2 Corinthians 6:2.) Notice that this scripture doesn't even say that "today" is the day; it says "now" is the day. The Greek word for "salvation" means "wholeness." It can also be translated "health." Its counterpart—the word for "save"—is often translated "heal" or "make whole." We are living in a time when God is expressing His favor in the earth. Jesus inaugurated this time of the Kingdom, healing all and then sending us to do the same. Miracles are a normal part of the Christian life, and we should always expect immediate results.

(3) Make opportunities. There's a difference between putting effort into ministering healing and making an opportunity for healing to happen. Too often we put in effort—trying to say the right words, feel the right feeling, or think the right thought. But all we need to do, as we have already discussed, is lay hands, follow the Holy Spirit's guidance, and completely trust Jesus to do all the rest. The more opportunities you make for a miracle, the greater the likelihood of it happening.

(4) Seek out good teaching. In Ephesians 4:11-13, Paul teaches us that Jesus has placed certain ministers in the Church for the purpose of training and equipping believers to serve God and people effectively. Their role is to teach and admonish us into unity so that the body of Christ—the Church—can mature. And the end-game is that we all attain "to the whole measure of the fullness of Christ." God can use sound teaching and training to make us more like Jesus—both in terms of our character and in terms of our faith-filled ministry to others. Be proactive about your transformation, and aim for the unbelievable target God has made available: the *whole* measure of the *fullness* of Christ.

(5) Trust and rest. Choose not to stress about it. Refuse to let the absence of a miracle have more authority over your emotions than the Holy Spirit does. Trust that God is faithful and that you are growing. God is conforming us into the image of Jesus. (See Romans 8:29.) That means every time you attempt to minister healing, you're more like Jesus than last time, which means it's more likely to happen this time than last time. Even if only ten seconds have passed since the last time you made an opportunity, you are now ten seconds more like Jesus than you once were.

When you apply these five principles to your

life, miracles become more common.

TAKING THE PRESSURE OFF

The question that couple asked me was mostly based on point number three above: making opportunities. How many opportunities should we make? And how long should we spend making those opportunities? How much is too much?

The message of wisdom that the Holy Spirit gave me was so simple. I looked at this couple who was holding hands as they sat on the front row of the church, and I asked, "Do you realize you're laying hands on each other right now?"

When Jesus healed the woman with the issue of blood, He wasn't paying attention. He wasn't trying to minister healing. He wasn't focused on the woman or even aware of her until after the fact. The only person who knew what was happening was the woman who thought that if she could just touch the hem of His garment, she would be healed. (See Luke 8:43-48.) I told this husband and wife, "If you will grab the hand of your spouse knowing that you're touching the body of Jesus, then he or she doesn't even have to be trying to minister healing; you can be healed simply because you've made contact with Jesus' body."

But the good news doesn't stop there. The story of the woman with the issue of blood is found in the middle of a story about a young girl who was sick and then died. Jesus came on the scene, raised her from the dead, and she was also healed. (See Luke 8:40-56.) One story is about a healing situation in which the minister was completely unaware, and the other was a situation in which the recipient was completely unaware. I said, "You can also grab your spouse's hand believing that Christ lives in you and wants to touch him or her, and they could be healed."

I added, "Keep it simple. You two could sit and watch a movie, holding hands just like you are right now, and experience healing simply because you're making contact with Jesus. If you'll hold hands in faith, then a miracle can happen."

The good news doesn't stop there either! In Acts 5:15, the people brought the sick out into the streets so that "at least Peter's shadow might fall on some of them as he passed by." Now understand, Peter didn't have a solar-powered healing gift, as though he ever had to say, "Sorry, everybody, it's cloudy today, so you're out of luck." The Greek language here simply means that people were being healed if they merely came into proximity of Peter. And I don't think Peter was solemnly marching down the street with his eyes half-closed and a super-spiritual air about him, waving his arms at the sick as he floated from one to the next. He was probably eating a loaf of bread and brushing crumbs off his robe. He was probably thinking about wherever he was going (much like Jesus when the woman with the issue of blood reached out and touched His garment).

Peter was probably just going about his day like a normal guy, and people were being healed as they came near him in faith.

I asked, "Do you realize you can be ministering healing to each other and seeking healing ministry from each other simply by being in the same house as each other?"

A lot of times, our only idea of healing ministry is an active session of purposefully laying hands on people and perhaps speaking commands to sicknesses and diseases. But that's only one form. Scripture also shows us passive healing ministry. Of course we need both, but you never have to feel bad stopping the active healing ministry because you can still minister passively. You also don't have to worry about frequency when you think of ministry as a constant part of life.

Think about it: In Acts 19:11-12, handkerchiefs and aprons that had touched Paul "were taken to the sick, and their illnesses were cured and the evil spirits left them." Can you imagine what's possible when you fold your family's laundry in faith? Or how about when you change their bed sheets? Or how about when you set the table or change the towels in the bathroom?

If you'll go about your day in faith that God's power can be rubbing off everywhere you go and in everything you do, then all of life becomes healing ministry to your family.

How Much is Too Much?

When you minister constantly in the ways I've described, you're left with only two guidelines for when to actively and purposefully minister to members of your family: (1) whenever the Holy Spirit specifically leads you, and (2) whenever the sick person requests it. Outside of that, you're under no obligation. Not only does this take the pressure off of you, but it takes the pressure off of your loved one.

No one wants to feel like a project. At a recent healing meeting, a man with advanced ALS attended in a motorized wheelchair. He had lost his ability to speak and was completely paralyzed. I wish I could tell you that he was healed when I ministered to him, but God met me where my faith was and still found a way to love the man through me.

The Holy Spirit spoke to me about who this man was before this disease affected him. It was as though I knew him for years (his parents and friends confirming everything I was saying). God revealed prayers the man had prayed as the disease set in and the desires he presently had in his heart to minister to others. Even though he couldn't move or speak, I could hear his heart as tears rolled down his face. This man wanted to minister to others more than anything else in the world.

The next day I held a question and answer session about healing ministry. The man I ministered to was unable to attend (the meeting was a long way from where he lived), but some other people from his church were there. One of them asked what sorts of activities they could do to help him seek healing.

I shared a lot of the points I've mentioned so far in this book, but I added one more. I said, "He wants to minister to people, and he doesn't want to feel like a project. He doesn't attend your small group so that every week everyone can practice on him. He attends your small group so that he can be part of the body of Christ. He's a believer, so Jesus lives in him. That means you can be healed when you touch the hem of his garment. He can't move or speak, but he still carries the presence of the Holy Spirit. If you need healing, grab his hand and talk to him. Tell him what's been happening to you and say, 'I know Jesus lives in you, so I'm holding your hand and expecting a healing out of this.' Ask him to pray for you too. His mind is sharp, and he knows how to pray even if his mouth can't make the words. Treat him like a fellow believer, not like a project."

Love sees Jesus in people and values them as more than a pet project. People can feel that, and they appreciate it.

When everything you do is healing ministry, people don't feel like projects; they just feel loved. Minister actively and purposefully whenever it's appropriate, but trust the overflow of the Spirit's work in your life to produce an atmosphere of healing in your home that never turns off.

Chapter 6

WHAT TO DO IF YOUR FAMILY MEMBER DOESN'T WANT TO BE HEALED

IF YOU HAVE ANY EXPERIENCE MINISTERING healing to strangers on the street, you've probably encountered people who aren't at all interested in letting you minister to them. It could be that they think you're trying to pull some sort of scam on them, or maybe they don't have time to stop, or maybe they legitimately think it's a waste of time. I've even encountered people who politely said something like, "No, my church is already praying for me" (the healing ministry equivalent of "I gave at the office").

But when it comes to family—especially people you're with on a daily basis—most of those excuses fall flat. To some of us, it seems unthinkable that someone might not want healing ministry, but understanding their reasons can help us more effectively love.

The first step in ministering to someone who doesn't want to be healed is finding out why. In this chapter, we'll look at several reasons people might reject ministry, and I'll offer a few pointers for how to proceed in each situation.

UNBELIEF

The first and most obvious reason is that they simply don't believe healing is possible. It may well be that the person would love to be healed if they thought such a thing was real, but they see that as nothing more than a fantasy and don't want to get their hopes up.

In these cases, let the person know that there is no requirement for them to believe it's possible. I like to say, "Jesus raised the dead, and dead people don't need to figure out how to receive. Dead people don't even have to believe anything. So if nothing happens, no biggie. But I want to at least give it a shot." This generally takes the pressure off the person, and often they're then willing to humor you. The best part is when you have that person test out their condition and they look at the former source of pain and then back at you with a confused look. Keep things low pressure at this point. I like to say, "Now, be honest, not polite. Is there any change?"

If the person is healed (and this goes for every scenario below as well), use it as a Gospel opportunity. Let the person know that their healing is proof that God has forgiven them of everything they've ever done wrong (See James 5:15.) Tell them that this proves Jesus has power to transform their entire life, not just their body.

If the person is not healed (and this also goes for every other scenario below), it's still a Gospel opportunity. I'll usually say something like, "Well, I'm going to keep praying for you and believing a miracle can happen because there are two things I know for sure: God loves you, and Jesus died on the cross and rose again so that you can be completely whole in your physical, psychological, and spiritual health."

CONCERN FOR YOU

A step up from unbelief is when the person doesn't even want to humor you by letting you minister to them, often because they are concerned for you. They don't want you to feel bad, they don't want you to be disappointed, and they don't want to reinforce what they feel are your "delusions."

One of the best responses in this scenario is to share testimonies of other people you've seen healed (assuming you have such stories). Then you can say, "Listen, I minister to people all the time who aren't healed, and it doesn't destroy me emotionally. But the people I have seen healed all have one thing in common: They all let me minister to them."

Another option is to simply reassure the person that this is just one way of showing that you care and want them well. If they still don't want you to minister, there are some backup plans we'll talk about in a bit that apply to any situation.

INSECURITY

Sometimes people don't feel like God loves them enough to heal them, and they feel that if they aren't healed, it will only prove He doesn't love them. Such people would rather such a painful notion be a mere idea than something they experience firsthand.

Be gentle with such people. Let them know that God's love for them is bigger than whether or not a miracle happens at this moment. God's love for them was proven two thousand years ago when Jesus left heaven, lived a sinless life among us, died to free us from sin, rose again victorious over death, and made a way for us to be transformed and experience an intimate relationship with Him on a deep, spiritual level. Eternal life is knowing the Father and the Son through union with the Holy Spirit. (See John 17:3

and 1 Corinthians 6:17.) That is a gift that transcends any miracle in the physical realm, and it is something that no sickness or disease can destroy. (See Romans 8:35-39.)

Once a person is secure in God's love for them regardless of the outcome, they'll be more likely to grant you permission to minister to them.

UNWORTHINESS

In Chapter Two, I briefly mentioned how often I run into people who don't feel like they deserve to be healed, to which I respond, "You're right, and neither does anyone else." The only thing we deserve is death. (See Romans 6:23.)

But the good news is that Psalm 103:2-3 says, "Praise the Lord, my soul, and forget not all His benefits—who forgives all your sins and heals all your diseases;" and then verse 10 continues, "He does not treat us as our sins deserve or repay us according to our iniquities."

The goal of your conversation with the person who feels unworthy is to take their eyes off of their own unworthiness and place them on Christ and His absolute worthiness. I like to say, "Jesus deserves everything for which He paid, and He paid the price with His own blood for you to be healed. Your worthiness has never been in question. Jesus is worthy, and that's what matters right now. For Him, it was all about His love for you; but for us, it's all about our love for Him. We don't want one bit of His sacrifice to go to waste. Jesus deserves for you to be healed."

I have also encountered people who feel like there are plenty of other people who have more serious conditions than they do. This is especially true if someone they love has a worse physical condition than they do. These people simply need to know that God doesn't have a quota to fill, after which He runs out of miracles. They also need to know that Jesus paid the same price for both them and the other person, which means both healings matter just as much to Him.

INNER WOUNDS

I can't even begin to tell you how many people I meet who have been mistreated by other people in healing ministry. I'll never forget a woman in West Virginia coming to me in tears, dragging her oxygen tank behind her. She said, "Thirty years ago, my pastor told me that the reason I still have this condition is that I have hidden sin in my life. I've been begging God for thirty years to tell me what that sin is, but He won't tell me. Why won't He tell me?"

I simply answered, "Because you don't have hidden sin in your life. Listen: the Holy Spirit wants you to be holy even more than you do. If you ask Him to show you sin in your life and help you to change, He's really good at helping out in that way. If

He's not telling you about it after all that asking, I'd say you have nothing to worry about." Then I ministered healing to her.

When people have been spiritually and emotionally abused by well-meaning Christians during healing ministry, they're less likely to want to receive any ministry from you. When they've been blamed time and again for their sickness, they're not usually interested in coming to you to receive more blame. They already feel terrible enough without your help.

But if you're gentle with them and assure them that you'll keep things low-pressure, they may warm up to the idea.

I sometimes say, "It's impossible for you to do anything wrong here. My job is to lay hands on you, Jesus' job is to heal, and your job is to just chill here while Jesus and I do our jobs." Minister in love and gentleness, keeping all the pressure off of the sick person. You may even minister emotional and spiritual healing without even realizing it.

FEAR

The most common thing people are afraid of is disappointment. It seems like such a small thing to many of us, but some people have experienced traumatic disappointments throughout their lives, and they recognize they can't emotionally handle another disappointment. Take your time with such people and tell them that there's no pressure for them to expect anything to happen. It may also be helpful to assure them that you're not worried about the outcome and will be emotionally okay if nothing happens.

Others fear relapse, which seems strange when you think about it. For these, I simply appeal to their present circumstances and say, "So what if it comes back? Wouldn't you rather be pain-free even for a moment?" Most will then admit that this isn't the only reason they don't want ministry, and you can move on to more substantive issues.

Still others fear a loss of provision or perhaps legal ramifications. If a person collects money from a government welfare program because of their disability, they may be afraid of the dramatic life change that will take place if they're healed. Will the government think they were faking their condition all along if they're suddenly fine? Their entire way of life could be in jeopardy. Or suppose the person is currently in a lawsuit because negligence on a company's part led to their injury. If that injury is healed, will the court rule against them? Will they lose their case and have to pay their legal fees out of pocket? I had one person reject ministry because they didn't want to lose their handicap parking privileges!

And then there are those who fear the unknown. I remember ministering to a seventy-something-year-old man who was in a motorcycle accident about forty years earlier and needed a cane ever since. When the pain left and his mobility started coming back, he started crying. I asked him what was going on, and he answered, "I just realized I have forgotten how to live any differently and don't even know what it will be like to not have this pain." The next day, I saw him without his cane and asked how he was feeling. He excitedly answered, "Last night I walked up the stairs in my house alternating my feet for the first time in forty years! It felt so good that I went back down and did it four or five times. I feel great, but my muscles are so sore!"

Whether a person fears disappointment, a relapse, loss of provision, legal consequences, or simply the unknown, sometimes all they need to know is that you'll be with them to navigate through those things just like you're with them now in their sickness. (That only works for family, of course. If you happen to run into one of these issues while ministering to a stranger or a loose acquaintance, you'll need to point out that God will continue to be with them to help them and that a local church would be a great place to go for more tangible help and counsel.)

PRIDE

I once ministered at a meeting where a man brought a friend who needed healing in his back. The friend was a veteran of the recent Iraq war and was honorably discharged because of an injury he suffered in combat. He had been awarded a Purple Heart medal—a prestigious honor for American soldiers who have been wounded in battle.

This former soldier didn't even want to be at the meeting and only came to humor his friend. The friend dragged him up to me and asked me to minister healing to his back. I did, but the man refused to even try to test out his condition. Most people will at least bend a little bit, but this man wiggled his shoulders and said nothing changed in his lower back. I convinced him to let me try one more time, but after that he didn't want to pursue it further.

For this man to be healed would be to lose his honor. His chronic pain was a source of pride for him.

Pride is perhaps the most difficult issue to confront because it values self over Jesus. The only solution is the Gospel. This man may have claimed to be a Christian, but the sad truth is that he valued his own sacrifice above Jesus' sacrifice. He valued his own honor above Jesus' honor. I never had the opportunity to speak to that man again, but I think I'd like to sit with him and talk about the beauty of the death and resurrection of Jesus, the majesty of who He is, and the joyous freedom of putting Jesus first in everything. Perhaps the seed of the Gospel will penetrate the hard shell of self-preservation and self-interest and draw him into a life of surrender to Jesus.

Whatever the case, the solution to pride is joyful proclamation of the Good News and exaltation of Jesus.

How to Determine Which Reason is at Work

There are basically two ways to find out why a person doesn't want to be healed: (1) Special revelation from the Holy Spirit or (2) simply talking to the person. Sometimes it's a combination of the two.

I always like to caution people never to form judgments out of the things they feel the Holy Spirit has revealed to them about others. Paul said that "we know in part and we prophesy in part." (See 1 Corinthians 13:9.) In other words, you don't have all the information and therefore can easily misjudge the situation (not to mention, it's possible that you didn't actually hear from God). Revelation from the Holy Spirit is only meant to help us love more deeply and minister more effectively—not to cast judgment on people or heap condemnation on them.

If you feel like the Lord may have revealed something to you about why a person doesn't want to be healed, first pray about it. Ask the Lord how He wants you to proceed. He may lead you to simply talk to the person about it. Or He may give you a prophetic word of encouragement that will strengthen that person's faith without actually exposing their shortcoming. He may even lead you to give the person some space while you minister in more passive ways, like we discussed in Chapter Five.

HOW TO MINISTER IN EVERY SITUATION

No matter what you find to be the reason a person doesn't want to be healed, continue to care for their physical needs. Love them. Serve them. Remember that whatever you do for them, you are doing for Jesus. Continue to minister in those passive ways described in Chapter Five, and let the person know you're praying for them so that if a miracle does happen, they know it came from God.

When all else fails, attempt resurrection. I know this sounds like I'm making light of a serious thing, but I truly mean it. If a person refuses healing ministry and ends up dying, you have a little bit of time available to try ministering to them when they are powerless to protest. Again, I don't say this as a joke—it may be a divine opportunity. Keep your mind on Jesus and His victory, and minister with simple trust just like you do for healing. I know many people who have seen the dead raised in Jesus' name, and all of them say it's no different than healing ministry. Speak with authority on behalf of Jesus and tell the person to wake up.

It also bears mentioning again that you should continue to work with doctors and medical professionals to provide the best quality care possible. If you take your time and love well, there are always ways to minister healing, even to those who don't want it.

Chapter 7

CARING FOR YOURSELF

I RIDE BETWEEN FIFTY AND ONE HUNDRED
airplanes every year. On every flight, either a video or
a live presentation instructs the passengers that if the
cabin loses air pressure, oxygen masks will be released
from the panels above each seat. You're then told that
if you have a child or someone else who needs
assistance with you, you need to first secure your own
mask before helping others.

When you're a parent, this goes against your
natural instinct. Many parents will protect their
children ahead of themselves. But how helpful are

you going to be to your child if you manage to put their mask halfway on and then pass out?

I have seen chronic illness destroy marriages, strain families, and burn people out emotionally. Many times, when families travel to my speaking engagements from multiple hours away, it's because they're at the end of their rope. They're worn out, beaten down, and spent. They just want the struggle to be over.

Some people feel guilty taking time off from care-giving because they know (or assume) that no one else can care for their loved one as well as them. Some are afraid of their loved one dying while they take a break. Others are afraid of their loved one misunderstanding their absence. Whatever the case, they stay on-duty 24/7 and often end up burning themselves out.

Those most able to help others in an emergency situation above 10,000 feet are those who put their own oxygen mask on first. And those who are most able to serve sick people in their families are those who take time to maintain their sanity, their emotions, their health, their friendships, their marriage, and their faith.

MAINTAINING YOUR SANITY

Depending on the severity of your loved one's condition, you may suffer from sleep deprivation, poor nutrition, isolation, or exhaustion. All of these can take a toll on your mental health. While most of us can handle short stints of extreme stress, our bodies and brains weren't designed to function under these conditions for prolonged periods.

Depending on your situation, you may have to find different strategies to allow yourself more time to rest and unwind (including, but not limited to sleep). Perhaps there's another family member or friend who can relieve you from time to time—if only for a few hours each week. If you have the financial resources, it may be helpful to hire someone to help with some of the household chores. If not, there may be someone from your church who is willing to come once a week to tidy up or do your dishes. Let other Christians know what your needs and abilities are, and be realistic about it. I can't guarantee that they'll help, but it's unlikely that they will if you never ask.

See if you can find a hobby that works with your lifestyle—something that can be quickly picked up and put down so that you can remain on-call when needed. Perhaps reading, sketching, crafting, etc. Find something you enjoy doing that gives you a sense of accomplishment from time to time (whether from finishing a book, a puzzle, a project, etc.). Decide early on whether it's better to include your sick family member in that hobby (which could be great for your relationship) or whether you need it to be your own thing.

Finally, find someone to whom you can vent your frustrations, but make sure it's someone who will also pray with you and for you.

MAINTAINING YOUR EMOTIONS

Along with the issue of maintaining your sanity is taking care of your emotional health. Since Jesus purchased your entire being—body, soul, and spirit—at the cross, it is illegal to willingly allow earthly situations to exert more authority over your emotions than the Holy Spirit. (See 1 Corinthians 6:19-20.)

If it weren't possible to exercise some level of self-control over your emotions, then Jesus, Peter, and Paul couldn't have commanded certain emotional decisions. Instead, they taught people to choose joy and peace in the midst of tremendous adversity.

> **John 16:31-33 –** "Do you now believe?" Jesus replied. "A time is coming and in fact has come when you will be scattered, each to your own home. You will leave Me all alone. Yet I am not alone, for My Father is with Me. I have told you these things, so that in Me you may have peace. In this world you will have trouble. But take heart! I have overcome the world."

> **1 Peter 4:12-13 –** Dear friends, do not be surprised at the fiery ordeal that has come on you to test you, as though something strange were happening to you. But rejoice inasmuch as you

participate in the sufferings of Christ, so that you may be overjoyed when his glory is revealed.

Philippians 4:4-7 – Rejoice in the Lord always. I will say it again: Rejoice! Let your gentleness be evident to all. The Lord is near. Do not be anxious about anything, but in every situation, by prayer and petition, with thanksgiving, present your requests to God. And the peace of God, which transcends all understanding, will guard your hearts and your minds in Christ Jesus.

No matter what you're facing in your earthly circumstances, the joy, peace, gentleness, and self-control of the Holy Spirit are freely available to those who will decisively turn to the Lord with thanksgiving and prayer, trusting Him to produce an emotional response that is aligned with heaven's perspective instead of earth's.

Heaven's perspective produces different emotional reactions than earth's perspective. In the Psalms, when the kings and rulers of the earth rise up and band together against God and His anointed (meaning King David, but comparable to us in Christ), God's response is laughter. (See Psalm 2:4) You can choose to join God in laughing at earthly problems because you recognize how tiny those things are in comparison to His limitless love, power, and goodness.

Maintaining Your Health

When you're on-call 24/7, sometimes it's easy for nutrition and exercise to take a backseat to the responsibilities of care-giving. Sometimes you can't get out of the house to shop for food and you instead end up ordering less-healthy food that can be delivered.

A lot of grocery stores now offer online shopping. Many will bring your cart out to your car at a scheduled time and will even load your car for you. Check with your local grocery stores to see if they offer such a service. You also might consider finding a friend or family member who will do the shopping.

It's also good to do some sort of meal planning. Healthy nutrition isn't only good for you as a caregiver; it may even help your sick loved one's condition improve in a natural way. But healthy nutrition doesn't happen on its own. Hunt down good recipes and consider the benefits of certain foods. Talk to your loved one's doctor about what would be best for their condition.

Also find time to exercise—especially in ways that will help you to be in your best shape for meeting your loved one's needs. Often this means needing strong core muscles in your back and abdomen (due to all the bending, twisting, and lifting that need to be done). Find some stretches and low-impact exercises so that you don't wear yourself out, and do them regularly to stay in shape.

If you need physical healing yourself, be careful not to fall into the trap of thinking it would be a bad thing for you to be healed before your family member. Many people feel guilty seeking healing for themselves when someone they love is in worse condition. But this isn't about you or the other person; it's about Jesus receiving everything for which He paid. Even if you're not concerned about your condition for your sake, be concerned about it for His sake. He wants you to be healed, and He isn't going to run out of miracles. If you're healed first, it will either stir up the faith needed for your loved one's healing or it will at least release you to be a more effective caregiver.

MAINTAINING YOUR FRIENDSHIPS

One of the hardest things to do when you become a primary caregiver for a sick family member is to maintain your friendships. Your schedule is now occupied at home, and your world now revolves around one person's struggle. If you're not careful, conversations with friends can end up being venting sessions, but that's only going to be good for a friendship when that friend welcomes it. Unfortunately, some people don't have the emotional fortitude to hear all that you're experiencing, and too much venting can cause them to back off and avoid you.

Try spending more time asking your friends

questions about their lives. If your friends don't
welcome venting, you'll need to find someone else for
that outlet—perhaps a pastor or Christian counselor.
When you talk about your sick family member, talk
about the victories. Talk about funny stories and
situations. In short, choose to be an enjoyable person
to be around.

You may even want to consider sending out
handwritten cards to people in which you encourage
them, pray for them, or share a prophetic word with
them. This could give you an outlet for ministry
outside of your own home, and it will keep you in
contact with people who love the ways you reveal
Jesus through your life.

I wish it weren't so, but most people are
subconsciously selfish and want to spend the most
time with those who they enjoy being around. If you
want to keep your friends, then keep being a
meaningful contributor to your friends' lives.

Maintaining Your Marriage

If you are married, you know what a strain
sickness can be on your relationship with your
spouse. This is compounded further if the sick person
actually is your spouse.

I remember a couple coming to one of my
meetings. The wife had a long list of health issues that
included chronic fatigue and fibromyalgia pain
throughout her body. They had traveled from several

states away to attend the meeting.

After ministering to the wife (who felt a little better but wouldn't know if anything really happened until later), I felt the Holy Spirit tell me that Jesus wanted to thank the woman's husband. I said, "Jesus wants to thank you for being faithful to your wife through all this. He knows it has been hard, and He knows you've lost hope in a miracle happening. He understands. He even knows that you didn't even want to drive to this meeting, but you did it because you love your wife." The man began to cry. I added, "It's okay. Jesus understands, and He's grateful to you for your love and endurance."

I shared more with him along the lines of what I wrote in Chapter Four—that his care for his wife is the thing that will matter at the final judgment. I told him he was on track to hear Jesus say, "Well done, good and faithful servant."

This man later confessed to me that he had been struggling in his marriage and contemplated leaving his wife. She was too tired and in too much pain to be intimate with him, and he was burned out doing all the work in the family. That prophetic word was exactly what he needed to hear.

Several months later, this couple came to another one of my meetings to tell me that the wife had been miraculously healed!

If your spouse is the one sick, find ways to communicate. Try to see if it is at all possible to be physically intimate with each other in a loving way, even if that just means kissing or holding hands.

If your spouse is not the one sick—perhaps you have a sick child, sibling, or elderly parent, for example—your husband or wife needs your time and attention just as much as your sick loved one. You may think that you are strong enough to handle the schedule you're living, but you are only as strong as what your spouse can handle. If your spouse says you are too busy, then you are too busy. Work together to find solutions and establish a good schedule. And I know some will scoff when they read this, but find a way to take a vacation together—even if it's just a romantic getaway where you decorate your bedroom like Hawaii or something. Go on regular dates—even if it's just a picnic on the floor of your basement. Find creative ways to be romantic, spontaneous, and fun even with the limitations of your schedule.

No matter who is sick, encourage and pray with your spouse regularly. Thank them for loving you. Give them your full attention for at least thirty minutes a day. It is possible to preserve your marriage in the midst of the struggle.

MAINTAINING YOUR FAITH

There are certain cliché messages that everyone expects from a teaching on maintaining your faith: Pray, read your Bible, stay connected with your church, etc. All those things are great components of the Christian life, and you should indeed make time for them throughout your day and week. But I want to talk about something deeper.

Jesus said in John 15:5 that apart from Him, we can do nothing. Only His Spirit can give us the strength, perseverance, and emotional strength we need to minister effectively to our family for any length of time.

The word "faith" means "active trust." We'll discuss this more in Chapter Ten, but for now, the thing you need to know is that you need to maintain your active trust in God.

It's easy to depend on your own strength, willpower, knowledge, or experience when caring for someone. But all these things have limits, and all these things can operate without love. Only the Holy Spirit can transform you into the beautiful expression of Jesus that you're designed to be, and He can only do it as you daily trust Him to live through you.

Prayer, Bible study, and church attendance mean nothing if we never actively trust the Holy Spirit to express Jesus through our lives. But when we do entrust ourselves to Him, then prayer, Bible study, and church attendance serve to strengthen our faith and help us to trust God even more, making us more like Jesus every day.

A secondary component is that when we truly trust God, we trust Him to work through other people as well. If you're the type of caregiver who feels like you're the only person who can take care of your loved one and you don't trust anyone else to do it, talk to the Lord about it until you have an assurance in your heart that He will empower another caregiver just like He empowers you.

Hebrews 12:2 instructs us to focus our attention on Jesus, calling Him the "pioneer and perfecter of our faith." The New Living Translation (NLT) renders this portion differently, calling Jesus "the Champion who initiates and perfects our faith." In other words, if you don't have faith, turn your focus to Jesus, and He will initiate it. And if your faith isn't perfect, look to Jesus; He will perfect it.

Chapter 8

PROCESSING SETBACKS AND LOSS

My FRIEND'S PARENTS WERE BOTH DIAGNOSED with cancer. This couple had been members of our church for decades, and the people of our congregation loved them deeply. They had hundreds praying and sometimes fasting for them. They traveled to every "faith healer" they trusted and sought out all manner of treatments. They repented of even the subtlest sins and believed with all their hearts that God wanted them to be healed. Eventually, the husband was set free, but cancer took the life of his wife.

While our study in this book is focused on how to expect miracles, I know that the trenches are messy. Sometimes we face setbacks that challenge our faith, and sometimes we even face the tragedy of loss.

If we're not careful, we can allow setbacks and the loss of loved ones to have more influence on our thinking than the love of the Father and the words of Scripture. In this chapter, I'm going to teach you how to continue fighting in simple faith even in the face of heartbreaking circumstances.

JESUS REVEALS THE FATHER'S HEART

The first thing we need to settle is the nature of God. When we understand God's heart, it's easier to view tragedy through the lens of His goodness.

A thorough study of God's nature would be far broader than the scope of this book will allow, so right now, I simply want to focus on how God views disease, death, and loss.

Scripture tells us that the only perfect revelation of the Father is found in Jesus, so any study of His nature must begin there.

> **Hebrews 1:3a –** The Son is the radiance of God's glory and the exact representation of His being...

> **John 6:38 –** For I have come down from heaven not to do My will but to do the will of Him who sent Me.

John 8:28-29 – So Jesus said, "When you have lifted up the Son of Man, then you will know that I am He and that I do nothing on My own but speak just what the Father has taught Me. The One who sent Me is with Me; He has not left Me alone, for I always do what pleases Him."

Jesus perfectly revealed the Father. Some people have the idea that the Father made people sick, and Jesus went around cleaning up His messes. But Jesus was "the exact representation" of the Father's being. He told Philip that anyone who saw Him had also witnessed the Father. (See John 14:8-11.) Jesus came to do the Father's will, not a separate will of His own.

In John 5:19, we learn that Jesus only did what He saw His Father doing. Isn't it interesting that Jesus didn't go around giving people tumors and diseases? Instead, He healed everyone who came to Him, called out to Him, reached out and touched Him, or had someone else petition Him on their behalf. Apparently, that's what the Father was doing as well.

Jesus never sent a suffering person away without the miracle they needed.

That's the Father's nature.

Did Jesus ever make anyone sick? The only case in Scripture where Jesus was personally involved in afflicting someone with a condition was when He appeared to Saul on the Road to Damascus and struck him blind. (See Acts 9.) This one and only case indicates that as long as someone wasn't on their way to murder and persecute Christians when they received their condition, it *probably* wasn't God who gave it. Regardless, God's prescription was that as soon as a Christian could come to Saul, that person's job was to minister healing. (See Acts 9:17-18.) Even when God brings the affliction, His desire is to heal.

> **Lamentations 3:31-33 –** For no one is cast off by the Lord forever. Though He brings grief, He will show compassion, so great is His unfailing love. For He does not willingly bring affliction or grief to anyone.

Even in the Old Testament, we see that God's heart is not to bring grief or affliction. It's not His will. His will is revealed through Jesus. And Jesus healed all.

GOD HATES DEATH

I have no question in my mind that God hates death. If He didn't, then why would He allow His own Son to be tortured and killed for the sake of providing us all with eternal life? Remember, Jesus perfectly revealed the Father's heart; and as far as we know from Scripture, He created problems at every funeral He ever attended when He raised the dead!

Even if we turn to the Old Testament, we can

find this fact. God is not a fan of death. It's not how He designed this world. All the way back in the creation story, we learn that death is the result of sin, not God's design. God doesn't like death.

> **Psalm 116:15 –** Precious in the sight of the Lord is the death of His faithful servants.

The Hebrew word for "precious" here means "costly" and "of great consequence." In other words, God doesn't like when His faithful servants die. We are of much more value to the advancement of the Kingdom here than we are in death. The death of believers is no small thing to the Lord. This verse even indicates that it breaks His heart.

"But that verse is about believers," you say, "What about evil people?"

Look at what God spoke through the prophet Ezekiel:

> **Ezekiel 18:23,32 –** Do I take any pleasure in the death of the wicked? declares the Sovereign Lord. Rather, am I not pleased when they turn from their ways and live? … For I take no pleasure in the death of anyone, declares the Sovereign Lord. Repent and live! (See also 33:11.)

God takes no pleasure in the death of the wicked. He is grieved along with us when people die.

First Corinthians 15:26 tells us that death is an enemy of God, and it will eventually be overthrown. Until that time, however, death is a reality we all face. Unless Jesus returns first, every human being is appointed to die at some time in this world. (See Hebrews 9:27.) But stories like Ananias and Sapphira in Acts 5:1-11 prove that God does not need a terminal illness in order to end our life.

People often challenge me that if what I say about God's will to heal is true, no one will ever die. But who says God needs a sickness or disease to separate your spirit from your body? In fact, if you study all of the people who were raised from the dead in Scripture, they all died early deaths as a result of sickness, disease, or a severe injury—not peacefully in their sleep.

When we can see that our loved one's condition is not God's will, it's a lot easier to contend for a healing. It also helps with how we process setbacks and loss.

GOD LOVES TO OVERCOMPENSATE FOR INJUSTICE

Imagine you buy a car, sign all the papers, and walk out to your new vehicle only to be car-jacked as soon as you open the door. Some thief takes off in your new car before you even have the opportunity to enjoy it. That would be an injustice! If you purchase something fairly but it is stolen from you, that is an injustice.

Jesus paid the price for every human being on the planet to be completely whole. (See 1 John 2:2.) That doesn't mean everyone is saved, but it does mean the price has been paid for everyone. When people die in their sins without having repented, this is an injustice to Jesus because He did not receive the reward of His suffering. The same is true when people die of sickness and disease. Jesus paid the same price to eradicate sickness as He did to eradicate sin. When sickness or disease seem to win a battle, it is an injustice, and God will bring retribution on the enemy.

Some of the most tragic human suffering in Scripture happened to a man named Job. His suffering arguably lasted no more than a year—perhaps only a few weeks. Satan killed his family, destroyed his home, took all his possessions, and afflicted him with terrible disease. But at the end of the story, God restored to Job double of everything that was taken from him and then blessed him with 140 years of long life to enjoy it all. (See Job 42:10-17.) God overcompensated for the injustice.

In Joel 2:25, God promised that He would "restore the years the locusts have eaten," which means not only that the famine would end but that the people would reap more than they could consume until they were paid back for everything that was taken. Here too, God overcompensated for the injustice suffered by His people.

The ultimate expression of God's

overcompensation for injustice is seen in Jesus on the cross: One innocent life that paid the price for all humanity to be saved.

If someone suffers a setback in their condition or dies while people are believing for a miracle, that's an injustice because Jesus didn't receive what He paid for. You can bank on the Lord's retribution.

Proverbs 6:31 says that if a thief is caught stealing, he must repay seven times what he took. Jesus said in John 10:10, "The thief comes only to steal and kill and destroy; I have come that they may have life, and have it to the full." Any setbacks or losses we face as we contend for miracles are the result of the thief—either through the enemy's direct activity or indirectly as a result of this fallen world, which goes back to the devil's work in the Garden of Eden. But Jesus came to destroy the devil's work. (See 1 John 3:8.) Jesus came to give us life "to the full." Jesus' first goal is to protect us from the thief. But if, for any reason, the thief gains the upper hand, Jesus will make him regret it.

Any time tragedy happens, expect God to bless you and your family and restore your hope. I don't know how long it will take or what it will look like, but I do know that He is faithful.

Remember that couple I mentioned who both had cancer? After the wife died, my time of processing the situation with the Lord led to me changing my mind about everything I had previously believed about healing theology and how to minister healing. Three months later, I began preaching with conviction that it is always God's will to heal—that Jesus paid for it and proved the Father's heart through His actions in His earthly life. Miracles started happening. From that time in 2009 until now as I write, God has used me to train tens of thousands of people to minister healing. I have witnessed thousands of miracles. I have taken the Gospel with a demonstration of power into some of the darkest regions of the world and led thousands to Christ.

My friend's mother's death was not in vain. I have lost contact with that family and don't know what God has done in their lives, but I know what He did in mine. God overcompensated for the injustice. Every time I lead a Hindu, a Muslim, or anyone else into total surrender to Jesus—every time I minister healing to another person with a terminal disease—every time I train an entire church to minister healing in Jesus' name—I believe Satan regrets fighting so hard to take that woman's life. I'm not saying this is my motivation for doing these things; my motivation is always Jesus and His sacrifice. But I am saying that God doesn't let one injustice go to waste when we determine to stand firm in our faith no matter what happens around us.

If your loved one suffers a setback, refuse to be discouraged. Instead, choose to be excited because the blessing is building up steam. Our just God will overcompensate with a greater blessing. And if your loved one dies while you're seeking a miracle, I understand that nothing can replace that person's life; however, God has not forgotten you and can turn the tragedy around to wreak havoc on the kingdom of darkness. God will turn around every situation to bring blessing to His children.

> **Romans 8:28 –** And we know that in all things God works for the good of those who love him, who have been called according to His purpose.

RESPONDING TO FAITHLESS
FRIENDS AND FAMILY

WHEN PEOPLE IN YOUR FAMILY DISCOVER THAT
you believe in miracles—and especially when they
hear about any claims of miracles happening through
you—there are six common responses: (1) mockery,
(2) skepticism, (3) judgment, (4) avoidance,
(5) confusion, or (6) hero-worship. None of these
responses require real faith in God.

The struggle of dealing with these six
responses to our faith is compounded when we're

contending for a miracle within our family that hasn't yet come. In this chapter, I want to address all six of these faithless responses both in terms of how people relate to our belief in healing and how they relate to situations where we're still awaiting a miracle for someone we love.

MOCKERY

I'm blessed to be in a family where my relatives have never mocked me for my belief in healing, but I know this is a unique privilege. Many believers face intense ridicule for their faith—especially when that faith goes beyond mainline Protestantism and actually expects God to be miraculously active today.

I hear many stories of people whose spouse, parent, or child is terminally ill and who are wrestling emotionally with friends and family who think they're insane for expecting a miraculous turnaround. When someone you love is given a terminal diagnosis and you choose to believe for a miracle, the doubters' responses range from, "Isn't that quaint," to, "Give it up, you lunatic, and face reality."

But I have seen far too many people healed in the midst of a terminal diagnosis. Our movie, *Paid in Full*, opens with the testimony of Troy Ritchie who had stage four brain cancer and was given only a few months to live. But God miraculously healed him. A friend of my family watched the movie with stage four prostate cancer and two or three months left to live. While he was watching, God healed him. That was over two years ago, and he's still alive and well today. I was recently at a meeting where a gentleman came who had been at one of my previous meetings a year earlier. At the time, he had stage four colon cancer that had spread into his liver. A few months after being at the meeting and receiving ministry from ordinary Christians who laid hands on him, he went in for his scheduled surgery to have a section of his liver removed. The man told me—now nine months later—that the doctors found absolutely no trace of cancer. Miracles are real, and our expectation of such things is no delusion.

Perhaps the greatest way to fight mockery is with sincerity and level-headedness. When people can see that you're not behaving erratically or as though you're in denial, it gives them pause. When people see you continuing to faithfully love and care for the sick person, providing the best quality of life that you possibly can, their mouths are often silenced by your selflessness.

Regardless of whether or not your sincerity shuts down the mockers, you can rejoice because you are experiencing part of the sufferings of Jesus. (See Mark 15:31-32.) Mockery is likely to happen, but if you're more focused on pleasing God than you are on pleasing people, you should be able to endure.

SKEPTICISM

While I haven't faced mockery for my belief in healing, I'm no stranger to skepticism. I have plenty of friends and relatives who do all they can to blame my testimonies on psychology or coincidence. They view me as someone who is genuine but probably either deceived or superstitious.

But psychology doesn't open deaf ears and blind eyes, and coincidence can't comprehend the odds of so many miracles happening at the moment someone laid hands on a person or spoke a command for healing.

When you're contending for a loved one's healing, skeptics will tell you that miracles are long-shots and are nothing more than rare coincidences, so you shouldn't wear yourself out expecting one. Sometimes I wonder if their motivation for saying this is that our belief exposes their own unbelief, and the most comfortable solution is to convince us not to believe. Whatever their motivation—whether self interest or genuine concern for our emotional and psychological well-being—the one thing most likely to convince the skeptic is the miracle happening.

I began healing ministry in 2009. I was healed of degenerative disc disease in 2011. For a year and a half, I ministered healing to almost one hundred people while I was still suffering with chronic pain. During that time, I had plenty of people—even pastors—question how I could be so convinced of

God's will to heal when I was still hunched over in agony. Skeptics aren't always found outside the Church; some have been Christians for years.

Your job remains the same: love. Love your sick family member, and love the skeptics. Answer their questions with gentleness. See if they have anything going on in their health that needs healing and minister to them. Many skeptics actually value the truth and aren't trying to be difficult. If you're patient, loving, and consistent, you may be able to win some of them over.

JUDGMENT

Judgment comes in all shapes and sizes. Some people assume that your belief in a miracle somehow means you're providing a lower quality of care for your loved one. This view is reinforced every few years when we hear a news report about some parents who are being charged with neglect for refusing medical treatment for their child who died while they believed for a miracle. But quality medical care and pursuit of a miracle are not mutually exclusive.

Other times, people judge your motives. Some of this plays into hero worship, which we'll discuss in a moment. There are those who believe you truly do have the ability to heal people in Jesus' name, and they feel personally insulted if you don't visit every sick person they know. They assume that you either don't care or that you have unbalanced priorities.

Along these same lines, some assume that you should spend all day emptying out hospitals instead of working a job or taking care of your family. Ironically, if you tell them that you can teach them to do the same things so that they can spend all day emptying out hospitals, they suddenly become disinterested. (Never mind the logistical problems and legal barriers involved.)

And in the saddest scenarios, as we discussed in Chapter Six, sometimes the judgment can come from the person to whom you're ministering. When people don't want to be healed, they can judge you to be some sort of fanatic or lunatic for always talking about healing. Some may even assume that you refuse to accept reality.

The challenge of judgment is that friends and family members who you love have beliefs about you that simply aren't true. People will judge your character, your motivations, and your actions. They may even gossip about you and spread their toxic perspective to others.

But there's only one Judge who matters. When you rest in the fact that He approves of you and that He truly does want this miracle you're pursuing, you begin to care less and less what other people think.

If we try to please people, we will run ourselves ragged; but if we aim only to please God, we can have a deep inner peace that transcends our earthly struggles and helps us to endure.

AVOIDANCE

Some friends and family will simply avoid you because they don't know what to make of your belief in miracles. It is easier for them to dodge the issue than face the questions in their own hearts.

A lot of these people are fellow Christians who either don't believe in healing or at least don't believe in it the same way you do. I know people who celebrate my missions work overseas and have donated to our orphanage project in Uganda but have no idea what to make of all the miracle testimonies.

If the person is a Christian, let them see your passion for the Gospel and your devotion to Jesus and the Great Commission. Find common ground on the basics of Christianity. Let them see your love for God and others. In time, they may warm up to the miraculous side of God that you know and trust.

If the person is not a Christian, don't push the miracle stuff. Bring them an entry-level Gospel that builds their interest. The more they see your genuine love and goodness, and the more they understand your testimony of what God has produced in your life, the more open to God's power they will become.

Usually the reason people avoid us is because they actually respect us but, for whatever reason, can't bring themselves to believe what we claim about the miraculous. In other words, if someone is avoiding you, don't take it personally. There's a good chance they think very highly of you and are just trying to escape the crossroads of decision that are forced by confrontations with the miraculous. Continue to love with low pressure, and continue to focus on the Gospel of salvation.

CONFUSION

Everybody has that one friend or relative who is into some form of Eastern religion or New Age mysticism. When this person finds out you believe in miracles, they're instantly convinced that you're on the same team. They want to talk about Reiki, healing crystals, or the law of attraction. They think you have a special gift or a strong aura that enables you to heal people. They probably believe in some form of "god" or "goddess" and believe Jesus is nothing more than a spirit being who you happen to channel to help people, but they are okay with you believing whatever you like if it's helping people.

What these people need most is the Gospel, but they're usually engaged in the beliefs they've adopted because they're not impressed with Christianity. Many have been wounded by Christians. Others were part of powerless churches that looked terribly unattractive when they discovered the power of their new belief system. Many of them even believe that they're doing good deeds, showing kindness, and using "good energy" or "white magic," so they don't understand your concerns about what they do.

But the issue is not the motivation or the

outcome; the issue is faith. Romans 14:23 says that "everything that does not come from faith is sin." Faith requires complete trust in God. All mysticism and New Age methods, however, require either trust in false gods (or spirits) or some sort of human effort. Even those who try to Christianize things like Reiki miss the point that they treat healing like a skill that can be developed. It's all about one's own ability to "channel energy"—not God's faithfulness to work a miracle when we simply trust Him.

The first time Satan tried to tempt Jesus in the wilderness, he suggested that Jesus should command a stone to become bread. If this were not possible for Jesus to do as the Son of God, then it would not have been a temptation. Jesus' response was to quote a scripture about listening to God's voice. (See Matthew 4:3-4.) Jesus refused to wield any special power apart from the Father's leading. He chose to be completely dependent on the Father and only did what He saw the Father doing. (See John 5:19.)

In the same way, we must refuse to be tempted into working miracles apart from complete dependence on Jesus. Jesus called such unauthorized activity evil. (See Matthew 7:21-23.) Those who practice such things—no matter how well-intentioned—have failed the first temptation of Christ and surrendered to the kingdom of darkness. Guard yourself against this subtle trap.

I wish this weren't true, but some of these people likely attend your church. And to show you

how subtle the deception can be, some of them
would absolutely shun anything to do with New Age
mysticism, witchcraft, or the occult. But even in their
Christianity, they have developed self-focused ideas
about how to channel and direct healing power
through their own self-discipline. Some use anointing
oil like a magic potion. Some go through superstitious
rituals—or make the sick people somehow perform—
before attempting their work of healing. No matter
how Christianized it looks, and even if it is done in
the name of Jesus, if the activity is based on self-
effort rather than Jesus' effort, then it is the work of
darkness. It is evidence of deception.

Those who have been confused by false
religions and false spirituality need to see the superior
power of selfless, effortless, simple faith, expressed in
love. They may want to give you pointers and advice,
but your response should be to say, "Thanks, but I
have confidence that God will move even more
powerfully if I simply trust Him to do the work."

HERO-WORSHIP

When healing miracles become normal
through your life, sometimes you'll encounter a friend
or relative who thinks you have special super powers.
It may not look as extreme as the term "hero-
worship" implies, but they think you are a special
agent of God who can do things other people can't.

As I mentioned earlier, this issue often goes

hand-in-hand with judgment because it's very easy to let down those who think too highly of us. It's not easy for me to travel the world most weekends while I have sick family members here at home. It's not easy for me to explain why it's right to sit in my office and write a book about ministering healing to family rather than sitting by a sick family member's bedside until they're well. Those who put us on unhealthy pedestals typically don't understand the principle of obedience to God or of being led by the Holy Spirit. They don't understand how God values multiplication or the fact that we can minister healing long-distance.

Such people also often don't understand how we can go around ministering healing to other people and yet still have a chronically ill person living in our own house. It's even worse if they are the sick person, wondering why you apparently have this special ability to help everyone else except them.

Our role is to boast in our own weakness and continually point to Jesus. I have no problem saying to friends and family that this ministry is often heartbreaking, very messy, and even at times confusing. I don't tell them these things to "play the martyr" but to let them know this isn't a special power I can wield or a gift that I can turn on and off. I let them know that I have more questions than answers, but one thing I do know: Jesus is the same today as He was in the time of the Bible. If it was His will to heal all then, then it's His will to heal all now. He doesn't change. So if someone we know and love isn't yet healed, the problem is not that Jesus said "no" but that the Church is still in the process of becoming fully like Him.

Another important component is to avoid the hero complex ourselves. We need to constantly make this lifestyle of ministering healing available for others, reminding them of John 14:12 and Mark 16:17-18—that healing ministry is the work of every single person who believes in Jesus. If the person doesn't believe in Jesus, this may start a great conversation. And if the person does already believe in Jesus, you may just help them to step into another layer of the lifestyle Jesus wants for them.

IN SHORT...

When you boil it all down, it's really simple: The faithlessness of others is overcome by a lifestyle of faith. No matter what opposition or obstacles we face, the solution is always simple trust in Jesus and letting Him shine through us with love, kindness, and faithfulness. This is how we open people's eyes to the truth behind what we do. And when we then share the Gospel with words, our message carries more weight because our faithless friends and loved ones can see the reality of what God is producing in and through our lives.

Chapter 10

SIMPLE TRUST AND
EXPECTING MIRACLES

I HAD JUST RETURNED FROM MY FOURTH TRIP TO
Uganda and noticed when I used the restroom that I
was apparently bleeding internally. I first figured that
maybe it was just a fluke thing, but the bleeding
continued. After a week or so, I became more
concerned. What if I had contracted a parasite or
something while I was eating in the villages?

The bleeding and some other complications
worsened a bit over the coming weeks and sometimes

included some cramping, but every once in a while it would look like the bleeding stopped and I would be fine.

If I'm really honest, I was afraid to go to the doctor. I don't like having tests run—especially in that region—and I was frankly becoming afraid that it might be cancer or something. I put off visiting a doctor for a year, hoping the problem would just go away on its own; but the bleeding, cramping, and other issues only intensified.

Almost exactly a year since I came home from Uganda and first noticed the problem, I had a colonoscopy. The specialist diagnosed me with Crohn's disease. Suddenly, several episodes from my childhood and my lifelong reactions to certain foods made sense. I had really been suffering my entire life, but the condition had only been bad enough to cause bleeding for about a year.

As I've mentioned, I'm not opposed to medical intervention, but I wanted to see if there were any natural solutions before I tried some heavy chemicals. I did my research, bought a bunch of supplements, and changed my diet fairly dramatically. The bleeding stopped, and the symptoms were minimized within a couple weeks.

Unfortunately, if I deviated from my diet or forgot my supplements, the symptoms all instantly returned. The natural remedies were only masking the problem, not solving it.

During this time, I continued traveling from

State to State and even around the world, preaching in churches and open fields about the saving and healing power of Jesus and His victory over sin, sickness, and the enemy. Sometimes I laid hands on people for healing while my own stomach was in agony. Some nights, I would be awakened in my hotel room by excruciating pain. I would pace the room or writhe in my bed for hours and then preach the whole next day.

Throughout all of this—both before and after the diagnosis—I knew God wanted to heal me. I knew Jesus had made it available and that my healing was two-thousand years overdue. My wife and I regularly laid hands on my abdomen and spoke healing in Jesus' name. Sometimes my boys did too. Several friends at church did the same. I understand the struggle of believing in healing while still experiencing a chronic, incurable illness. I sometimes struggled in my thoughts, but it never shook my faith.

Defining Faith

Faith is active trust. Faith is not the same thing as belief. My favorite example is to say that I have faith in my wife. If she says she will meet me somewhere, I know she will be there. But if I instead believe with all my heart that she will arrive somewhere else, that's not faith. It doesn't matter how much I believe or expect something different, she is going where she said she would go.

Belief is based on information, which may or

may not be true. Faith is based on a person, who may or may not be trustworthy. God is always trustworthy, which means we can always entrust ourselves to Him.

One of the areas in which my wife is trustworthy is that she's a great mom. She takes amazing care of my two boys. Hebrews 11:1 says, "Now faith is the substance of things hoped for, the evidence of things not seen" (NKJV). I can be inwardly confident about my wife's parenting skills, but you can't see that. My faith is found in the fact that I travel the world—often for weeks at a time—and entrust my children to my wife. That active trust gives substance to my intangible hope and belief. It offers evidence of the trust in my heart that you wouldn't be able to see any other way. Faith without action is dead. (See James 2:14-26.)

Now suppose I believe with all my heart that my wife is a fantastic mother (which I do), but instead of ever entrusting my kids to her, I choose to hover over her shoulder and micromanage everything she does. Am I actually putting any faith in her? Not at all. My right belief is nullified and rendered irrelevant by my actions. Faith is the activity of placing trust in someone. Faith is visible.

But let's reverse that example for a moment: Imagine I thought my wife was a terrible mother and would neglect and abuse my children, yet I still traveled around the world and left them in her care. Is that an act of faith? Did I put faith in my wife?

Yes.

And that's great news for those of us who struggle with doubts and questions. Some of us disqualify ourselves from ministering healing because we spend more time analyzing our beliefs and doubts than we spend time analyzing the faithfulness and trustworthiness of Jesus. And because of this, we don't think we can make an opportunity for a miracle. We don't think we're allowed to lay hands on the sick or speak with authority because we think our unbelief disqualifies us.

Your doubts only disqualify you if you allow them to rule your actions. It would be much harder for me to entrust my kids to my wife if I believed she wouldn't take care of them, but it wouldn't be impossible. Faith is found in the action, not in the feeling. And lest you think that isn't true, remember that the entire Christian life is about doing what is right despite how we feel (until the Spirit more fully transforms us into people who feel like doing what is right).

Faith is simple trust expressed through action. Even if you don't know if you can trust God—even if you aren't sure whether or not He'll come through—keep laying hands on the sick until you see a breakthrough. This is the place where faith is grown.

KEEP IT SIMPLE

In Romans 12:2, Paul warns us not to conform to the patterns of this world. Instead, he says, we should "be transformed" by having our minds renewed. Faith-filled Christianity involves learning to think differently than the world thinks.

The world studies problems; the Kingdom of God studies the Solution. The world relies on self-will and human effort; the Kingdom of God relies on the Father's love, the Spirit's power, and the finished work of Christ.

In the world, if you try something and see no results, you either give up or try harder. If you can't unscrew the lid from the mayonnaise jar, you exert more strength, you beat on it with a knife, or you find some sort of jar-opening tool that can provide more leverage. But in the Kingdom, everything works by grace through faith (this is the point where I hand the mayonnaise jar to my wife, and she opens it immediately.) In the Kingdom, if something doesn't work, we try less and trust more.

Before I realized this principle, I tried to minister healing while thinking like the world. When my childlike prayer didn't heal the person, I assumed I wasn't trying hard enough. So the next time, I would squint my eyes really tight and try to push power out my arm. Since that didn't work, I assumed it must be harder still; so I would try to quote every Scripture about healing that I could remember. Since that didn't work, I figured it must be even harder; so the next time, I would smear oil on the person and jump and shout. And since that failed too, the next time I would fast for three days and then dump a larger quantity of oil on their head. Before long, I was running out of new things to try (and out of oil), and the people to whom I ministered were tired of my antics!

If we approach healing ministry like the world, then we will wear ourselves and the sick person out. Your family member is not your guinea pig. He or she is someone you and Jesus both love dearly—a human being who needs to feel more like a person than a project, as we discussed in Chapter Five.

If we approach healing ministry with a renewed mind—thinking like citizens of the Kingdom who trust our good Heavenly Father to do as He has promised—we are likely to see greater results. The less pressure you put on yourself, the better. The less trust you put in your own performance and the more trust you put in Jesus' sacrifice and victory, the more likely a miracle is to happen.

If you try to minister healing to your loved one and don't see results, don't sit around trying to figure out a way to put more effort into it. Instead, try less and trust more.

GRATITUDE

Paul wrote in Philippians 4:6, "Do not be anxious about anything, but in every situation, by prayer and petition, with thanksgiving, present your requests to God." Gratitude is an antidote for anxiety. As we thank God for the things He has done in the past, we are reminded of what He is able to do in the future. And as we thank Him in advance for what we trust Him to do in the future, we find the confidence to put faith in Him in the present.

As you pursue your loved one's miracle, take time each day to thank God for specific things you have seen Him do. Praise Him for who He is and thank Him in advance for the miracle you're expecting. Don't do this as an empty ritual or as an attempt to twist God's arm. Do it as a means of engaging your heart and mind in the Truth.

SHARE THE LOVE

I encourage people not to put all of their eggs in one basket when it comes to healing ministry. Something that often happens when a close family member is sick is that we allow that person to consume all our attention.

Some people feel guilty ministering to others—especially to strangers—when someone they love dearly is in so much agony. Many times I receive e-mails from people who are frustrated and worn out because they've been seeking a miracle for their spouse or child for years but have seen no results. Many of these same people admit that, although they may have prayed for other people, they've never tried actually ministering healing to anyone else in the simple way they've learned. They've studied healing, they've listened to hours of teaching, and they've "watched all of my YouTube videos" looking for answers that will unlock healing for their loved one; but they've never applied what they learned outside of their own home.

If we will realize who we are in Christ and what we carry, and if we will make opportunities for others to be healed, miracles will become normal. In that environment, our faith will both sustain and grow while we continue pursuing the miracle for our loved one.

Often the people who study healing ministry the most fervently are people who either need healing themselves or have someone in their life who needs to be healed. The kingdom of darkness wants nothing more than to take the people who carry the most revelation about healing and focus all their attention on one person—especially when that person is either their own self or a close family member (because of all the unique difficulties we discussed in Chapter Two).

If those believers would minister to people outside their own household—people for whom they don't need to overcome any emotional or relational challenges—hundreds more healings could take place. And if you think about it, we might actually start crossing paths with each other. In other words, imagine if you and I both had a sick family member for whom we were struggling to see a breakthrough, but we were both out ministering to others and ended up ministering to each other's family members.

Without those relational obstacles to overcome, we might even bring the breakthrough that the other was seeking in the first place, and it might even happen faster than if we had fought on our own!

My point is simply this: If you only ever minister to one person, then you will only ever see one miracle (if that), and you will miss thousands of opportunities to grow your faith and see other people set free.

NEVER STOP SEEKING

Finally, I want you to understand that your pursuit of a miracle is not selfish. Some people feel bad seeking healing for their loved ones because they're afraid that deep down they're just looking for an escape from all the work of providing care. Even if that actually is your motivation right now, shift your focus to the finished work of Jesus. Remind yourself that the King you love paid such an incredibly high price for your family member to be healed, and He deserves everything for which He paid.

When we keep our eyes on Jesus in this way, our pursuit of a miracle becomes an act of worship because we are seeking for Jesus to receive what He paid for. Anytime you seek healing—whether for yourself or someone else—it can be an act of worship. Whenever we seek for Jesus to receive the reward of His suffering—whether through evangelism, healing ministry, or our own personal transformation—it is an act of service for our King. It is worship.

Jesus said, "Ask and it will be given to you; seek and you will find; knock and the door will be opened to you. For everyone who asks receives; the one who seeks finds; and to the one who knocks, the door will be opened." (See Matthew 7:7-8.) The only way to not receive is to stop asking. The only way to not find is to stop seeking. And the only way the door stays closed is if you stop knocking. Perseverance is biblical.

From eight-years-old until thirteen, Sherry Sam's daughter suffered from regular seizures. Today, she has been seizure-free for six years and is doing the one thing she never thought she would do: driving a car. Sherry says, "Perseverance and simple faith are what worked for us. Simply believe. You don't need to earn a healing."

Fix your mind on the goodness of God, and persevere no matter the earthly circumstances. That's what my family and I did when it came to Crohn's disease. We continued believing God wanted me well, and we all determined to continue serving Him no matter my condition.

In June of 2015, I wrote an article on my blog at SupernaturalTruth.com titled "How to be Healed by Jesus." (I have included this article as an appendix in this book because you may find it helpful when ministering to your family.) In it, I mentioned my battle with Crohn's disease, letting the reader know that I was in this fight alongside them and wasn't preaching at them from some unrealistic place.

When that blog post went out to my email list, I received scores of replies in which people did exactly what I had taught them to do in the past. They wrote back various forms of, "Be healed in Jesus' name."

In that moment, I decided to take the advice of the article, which was to believe that absolutely any Christian can deliver the miracle you need. I had taught that all you really need is an encounter with Jesus, and even the least likely believer is still part of His body. I read those emails as though Jesus Himself were writing to me.

The next day, my symptoms were 80% better. After a couple more days of feeling fairly good, I decided to stop taking my supplements. By the time a month had passed, the symptoms were completely gone. I even stopped my special diet and found that I was completely healed. The "incurable disease" that had plagued me for three decades of my life was gone.

Refuse to give up on your loved one's healing. Refuse to back down on ministering healing to others. Continue serving Jesus no matter your circumstances and no matter the cost. Love well, and continue placing simple trust in the Lord.

Conclusion

HEALING MINISTRY IS SIMPLE. THAT SENTENCE tends to frustrate people because we don't always see immediate results. If it's so simple, they argue, why don't we see miracles every single time we touch a sick person?

I don't say it's simple because it's so easy for us to do. It is actually impossible for us to do apart from Jesus. (See John 15:5.) I only say it is simple because every single miracle I have witnessed—roughly four thousand in the last six years—has required no effort from anyone except Jesus. Every miracle has flowed out of simple trust. My statement that "healing ministry is simple" is meant as a reminder to not overcomplicate things.

In this book, you've learned:

- ➤ how to minister healing,
- ➤ how to identify and overcome challenges in ministering to family,
- ➤ how to trust other believers to carry the responsibility for your loved one's healing,
- ➤ the value of caring for the sick,
- ➤ realistic boundaries and techniques for ongoing healing ministry,
- ➤ how to work with family members who reject healing,
- ➤ how to care for yourself,
- ➤ how to overcome setbacks and loss,
- ➤ how to respond to people who faithlessly object to your pursuit of a miracle, and
- ➤ how to contend for a miracle.

This book isn't a comprehensive guide to healing ministry, but you do now know everything you need to know to pursue your loved one's healing.

In Jesus name, I pray for you right now that you will know the hope to which you have been called—that you will see what God has invested in you and that you will minister healing with confidence and simple faith. I pray that everything you have learned in this book bears fruit that will last. I bless your ministry to others and agree with you right now for your loved one's healing. May you see more miracles happen in your lifetime than you ever dreamed possible.

Appendix A:

HOW TO BE HEALED BY JESUS

The following is the article referenced in Chapter Ten that I wrote June 22, 2015—shortly before being healed of Crohn's Disease. You may find this helpful in pursuing your own healing or in helping your loved one navigate their search for a miracle. Some of the material has already been covered in this book (though this may be a good refresher, and it may be helpful to see it presented for the sick person rather than presented for a family member, as the rest of this book is).

Original Source:
http://supernaturaltruth.com/how-to-be-healed-by-jesus/

HAVE YOU EVER WONDERED HOW TO BE HEALED by Jesus? Perhaps you're suffering with a physical condition right now and have been begging God for relief. I want to offer you some practical advice about what to do next that I believe will lead to your healing.

In the last couple weeks, I've received close to 30 e-mails asking, "What am I doing wrong? Why am I not yet healed?" These dear people from all over the world tell me heartbreaking stories of all the things they've tried in their pursuit of physical healing. Some of them ask me to tell them more details of my own healing experiences, hoping to find a secret key that will unlock their own healing.

I get it. I've been there. And I don't fault anyone for asking such things.

But if there's one thing I've learned, it's that while the actual event of healing happens in an instant, there is often a long journey to reach that place. Even when Jesus was physically walking the earth, there were some who merely reached out and touched His cloak while others had to shout past naysayers, travel from surrounding villages, hike around a lake when He sailed away, or even chase Him down. Every account is different, and there don't appear to be any formulas for how to be healed by Jesus. The only common denominator—in every case—is Jesus Himself.

Before I continue, I want you to know that this article is going to tell you how to be healed by Jesus. But I also want to warn you: It may make you frustrated, and it may not produce instant results (I say "may," though, because I have seen this work so many times).

First, a little encouragement…

I'm In This With You

Many people know the story of how the Lord directed me to minister healing to myself when I had scars all over my face from second-degree sunburn. What was medically impossible actually happened within only one month of contending for my own healing. That was back in 2002. Many also know about how I was healed of degenerative disc disease in 2011 after suffering with chronic (and sometimes crippling) back pain for 4 agonizing years. A few even know about the time around 2005 that Jesus came to me in a dream and both healed and restored my teeth that had been literally falling apart (probably the most painful month of my life).

I know what it is to suffer while believing for healing, and I know what it is to experience the miraculous relief that comes when Jesus finally receives what He purchased.

What many do not know is that a few months ago, I was diagnosed with yet another condition for which I am still seeking healing.

I'm sometimes stubborn about seeing a doctor, so I went a year suffering with progressively worse cramps and even bleeding in my digestive tract until finally seeing my physician about my condition. When all the tests were complete, I was diagnosed with Crohn's Disease—an inflammatory bowel disease that attacks (in my case) the colon and causes serious pain, cramping, ulcers, and malnutrition (among many other things).

Even though I've been healed of more things than I can recount, and even though in a few of those cases I was able to minister healing to myself, I obviously don't have a "secret key" that will unlock a healing at-will. It just doesn't work that way. But don't let that discourage you because I do know what to do in order to be healed, and I'm actively practicing it every day, knowing that breakthrough is inevitable if I will persevere. And you can do this too!

The Healing is Found in the Healer

If I want to interact with my wife or receive a gift from her, there is no "secret key." I don't have to say a magic string of words like "pretty please with sugar on top" before she will bake me a cheesecake (which she did for Father's Day, and it was spectacular!). I don't have to beg her, kicking and screaming until she hears me and gives me something I want (like my 4-year-old has been doing for a Buzz Lightyear toy that may never materialize until he stops freaking out about it… A good father doesn't let his kids benefit from that sort of behavior!).

My wife loves me. She wants to care for me. And she knows that I love her and want to care for her. The ways in which we communicate are not attempts at pushing the right button to make the other do what we want. In fact, if I always approached her in the same way just to use her for my own purposes, not only would it become annoying to her but it would indicate that I don't really understand the relationship we have or how much she loves me.

In the same way, you don't need to figure out a secret method to approaching God. He invites us to enter *boldly* to the throne of grace — not cautiously with a choreographed dance under fear of being rejected if it isn't perfect.

Many have preached that "God is not a vending machine." Many who say this are trying to say that sometimes God doesn't want to heal us. To put it bluntly, that's garbage that is easily debated from a New Testament perspective. But on the positive side, the larger point being made is that God is not an inanimate object that we can control. Whenever we try to control Him, He reminds us that He is God. He's not a force to be manipulated. We can't twist His arm. And accordingly, the "secret key" that most of us are looking for simply doesn't exist.

What moves God's heart is not the right amount of tears or complaints (not that He ignores such things). What moves His heart is when we connect with Him as children to a loving Father. Sometimes that may come with tears and frustration as we make known our complaint to the Lord, so don't think I'm talking about a method of prayer. If we start talking methods, then we've missed the point again. He's our heavenly Dad, and He truly is a good and loving Father who loves to give good gifts to His children.

Your healing is not a special gift locked away in a box until you perform the right action and receive it as a reward. That's not a real gift. That's not grace. Grace implies a free gift (Clarification: It's free to you but was incredibly costly to Jesus).

Your healing cannot be sought as a secret treasure to be unlocked. Your healing is found in Jesus. He's the One who does the work–not you. He's the One who unlocked your healing 2,000 years ago. You don't need a secret key; you need Jesus. And if you're a Christian, then you already have Him.

TIME TO REST

Speaking as someone who has been healed of many "incurable" conditions yet is also presently suffering with one, I want to share with you the secret to my endurance, which has led to one breakthrough after the next. There's a reason I can stand in front of scores of people a few times a month and proclaim with absolute certainty that God wants to heal them immediately while my own gut is still twisted in pain. There's a reason I can walk through the grocery store with stomach cramps yet stop to boldly minister healing to a fellow shopper with a cane.

The secret to my perseverance is threefold:

(1) I refuse to give my physical condition more authority over my emotions than I give the Holy Spirit.

Your spirit and your flesh almost always want two different things. Christianity is all about choosing what the Holy Spirit has awakened your human spirit to desire versus what your flesh feels like saying, thinking, doing, or feeling. My life-circumstances do not have permission to dictate how I feel. The junk of life's struggles may try as hard as possible to take me down, but I try as best as I can to only offer the Holy Spirit the authority to rule my emotions. Sure, I may slip from time to time and catch myself feeling discouraged or worn out, but the overall disposition of my life is one of righteousness, peace, and joy in the Holy Spirit–the three indicators of God's rule and authority (Romans 14:17).

(2) I refuse to give my physical condition more influence over my theology than I give Jesus (as He is revealed in the Bible).

My back was healed in 2011, but I started operating in healing ministry more than a year and a half earlier in 2009. During all that time, I was ministering healing to other people — even watching other backs being healed in front of my own eyes — while

I myself was still popping Vicodin and Ibuprofen every few hours to make it through the day. I was convinced of God's will to heal — not because of how I felt but because of what I saw to be true in the Scriptures. From that time until now, I have refused to compromise the message of the Gospel for the sake of reconciling my own physical condition. And while I'm not yet healed of my current condition, my long-term observation has been that this is the right course of belief.

(3) I know that all my works and efforts are completely meaningless in achieving healing, and I simply need to rest in what Jesus has already done.

As mentioned already, healing comes by grace. It is a freely-given gift. If I start wondering what I'm doing wrong or what else I have to do to be healed, then I have lost sight of grace. I don't have to pray enough, fast enough, cry enough, beg enough, shout enough, dance enough, or *anything else* enough. If I focus on all those things, not only will I exhaust myself, but I'll be seeking healing from the wrong god–a god who dangles healing over my nose like a doggy-treat, not releasing it until I jump through the right hoop. I don't need to perform for the true God. He already paid the price on my behalf.

All I need is to touch Jesus.

HEALING COMES FROM TOUCHING JESUS

If there's any secret key to how to be healed by Jesus, it's actually no secret at all. It's clearly shown throughout the Biblical account of Jesus' life and ministry. If you want to build your faith a little, read the following verses while observing the common element among them all:

> **Matthew 8:3** — Jesus reached out his hand and touched the man. "I am willing," he said. "Be clean!" Immediately he was cleansed of his leprosy.

> **Matthew 8:15** — He touched her hand and the fever left her, and she got up and began to wait on him.

> **Matthew 20:34** — Jesus had compassion on them and touched their eyes. Immediately they received their sight and followed him.

> **Mark 1:40-42** — A man with leprosy came to him and begged him on his knees, "If you are willing, you can make me clean." Jesus was indignant. He reached out his hand and touched the man. "I am willing," he said. "Be clean!" Immediately the leprosy left him and he was cleansed.

Mark 6:56 — And wherever he went—into villages, towns or countryside—they placed the sick in the marketplaces. They begged him to let them touch even the edge of his cloak, and all who touched it were healed.

Mark 7:33-35 — After he took him aside, away from the crowd, Jesus put his fingers into the man's ears. Then he spit and touched the man's tongue. He looked up to heaven and with a deep sigh said to him, "Ephphatha!" (which means "Be opened!"). At this, the man's ears were opened, his tongue was loosened and he began to speak plainly.

Luke 8:44-46 — She came up behind him and touched the edge of his cloak, and immediately her bleeding stopped. "Who touched me?" Jesus asked. When they all denied it, Peter said, "Master, the people are crowding and pressing against you." But Jesus said, "Someone touched me; I know that power has gone out from me."

Luke 22:51 — But Jesus answered, "No more of this!" And he touched the man's ear and healed him.

Matthew 14:35-36 — And when the men of that place recognized Jesus, they sent word to all the surrounding country. People brought all their sick to him and begged him to let the sick just touch the edge of his cloak, and all who touched it were healed.

Luke 4:40 — At sunset, the people brought to Jesus all who had various kinds of sickness, and laying his hands on each one, he healed them.

Luke 6:18b-19 — Those troubled by impure spirits were cured, and the people all tried to touch him, because power was coming from him and healing them all.

Never once did Jesus turn someone away. Never did He say, "I'm sorry, but it's not My Father's will." Never once did someone touch Him with expectancy and walk away unchanged.

In Jesus' ministry, healing was a fact. If you touched Jesus, you were instantly and miraculously healed.

WHAT YOU DO *NOT* NEED TO DO TO BE HEALED

Again, please note the place from which I am writing to you: I have been healed many times, but I'm still suffering with a condition that has not yet experienced the touch of Jesus. The advice I'm about to give you is not a magic wand that you simply wave over yourself to receive a healing. But it is the one and only biblical prescription for how to be healed.

Can healing come in other ways? Absolutely. Again, it's not about a method. But what I'm about to share is the only biblical responsibility for a sick person.

Before I get to that, I want to make sure you know everything the Bible does NOT require a sick person to do:

(1) The Bible does not require you to have faith for your own healing

Only about a quarter of the time in the Biblical accounts did Jesus say, "Your faith has healed you." Other times, people were healed by the faith of others (like the centurion's servant or the Syrophoenecian woman's daughter). Still other times, the only person who had faith in a situation was Jesus. For example, when the epileptic boy wasn't healed, Jesus didn't blame the little boy. He didn't blame the little boy's dad. He didn't blame the surrounding crowd, even though He identified them as an "unbelieving and perverse generation." Instead, He placed the responsibility squarely on the disciples who were there to minister in His name (Matthew 17:14-20).

If you're healed, then someone had faith (maybe you, maybe someone else). But if you're *not* healed, then no one had effective faith in that specific situation. While it's not okay that you're not yet healed, it *is* okay in that it was never your responsibility to have the faith for your own healing (nor is it your family's responsibility, as noted above about the epileptic boy's dad). The only person who needs to figure out where their faith was lacking is the non-family person who ministered to you. We — the Church — are still in the process of growing "into the whole measure of the fulness of Christ" (Ephesians 4:11-13). Accordingly, we're still collectively growing into the faith needed to see everyone healed like Jesus did.

If you do have faith for your own healing, awesome! But even in Jesus' own ministry, that only happened a minority of the time. It's great when it happens, but it's not common, nor does Jesus require it. (In case you're wondering, yes I am saying that I have yet to exercise faith for my own healing of Crohn's disease, and I'm perfectly okay with that. It's admittedly a lot easier for me to have faith for other people to be healed than it is for myself, and I know Jesus understands that and doesn't fault me for it. It's actually liberating knowing that I don't have to figure out how to have faith for my own healing. When you're presently the one feeling a symptom — especially a painful one — it's hard to see that thing as tiny and conquerable by a simple touch or command of healing. That's why we need others to minister to us.)

(2) The Bible does not require you to confess promises or quote Scriptures

Please understand my heart with this one: There's absolutely nothing wrong with rehearsing the promises of God concerning healing. In fact, that's a GREAT thing to do, and there are many testimonies of people being healed after a season of praying and proclaiming God's Word concerning healing.

Nevertheless, I often receive questions asking, "What Scriptures am I supposed to be claiming?" or, "How many Scriptures do I need to memorize, and how often am I supposed to quote them in order to be healed?" These questions point to the underlying problem we've been addressing all along: You don't need to twist God's arm or perform for Him before He will heal you. Healing can't be earned. Healing is a gift. It's one thing to renew your mind and strengthen your faith with Biblical promises; it's another thing to treat those promises like magical mantras that will somehow move God's hand. So while this can be a good thing for you, it's not something the Bible says you need to do in order to be healed. Feel free to do this, but check your motives. You can't earn a healing, and Jesus never made someone quote a scripture before He would heal them.

(3) The Bible does not require you to uncover secret sins or spiritual roots to your condition

Something that often happens in Christianity is that we like to make practices out of experiences. For example, when we read that Jesus once spit in the dirt to make mud and then rubbed it into a blind man's eyes to heal him, we now find ourselves wondering — as we lay hands on a blind person for healing — whether we should try the old mud trick to achieve a breakthrough. (I don't recommend it. Try rubbing mud in your own eyes sometime and you'll find out why!) We want to turn every testimony into a formula because we think it will produce repeatable results. So when we learn that someone was healed of cancer after repenting when the Lord revealed hidden bitterness in their heart from years earlier, we then assume that every case of cancer requires such a revelation before it can be healed.

We're designed to look for and notice patterns. That's great when we're dealing with matters of science and the natural forces of the universe, but it's nonsense when we're dealing with a Person (anyone who has ever tried to figure out the opposite sex knows this!). Just because a specific thing led to God's healing touch before doesn't mean it necessarily will again.

As a matter of fact, James 5:15 indicates that when God heals a person, any sin in their life is automatically forgiven. Admittedly, verse 16 seems to present the opposite — confession first, followed by healing. In my observation both options are correct. I like to say that the blood of Jesus is messy: If you get a little on you for one thing, it's there for the rest. Confess sin first and then be healed, or be healed first and then forgiven. Both are biblical, but neither is required.

Bottom line: Jesus never made someone confess a sin or figure out a root cause before He healed them. All He did was touch them or speak a word of command. And it always worked. You don't need to figure out root causes in order to access your healing. If the Lord reveals something, great. If He doesn't, then it isn't necessary.

(4) The Bible does not require you to minister healing to yourself

This is perhaps the most important one. Again, I have ministered healing to myself, and I have seen many others successfully do so as well. But there is not a single passage in the Bible that prescribes such a thing. It's not expected. All that is expected is that we touch Jesus.

HOW TO TOUCH JESUS

The only consistent thing we can find throughout Jesus' healings is that Jesus was involved. Technically speaking, He didn't even need to have physical contact with a person for them to be healed — as the Centurion noted, He only needed to speak a word of authority (Matthew 8:8-9). But the most common method we see is physical contact with Jesus, or even the edge of His clothes.

Today, Jesus is physically in heaven, seated at the right hand of the Father. It would be impossible — apart from a miraculous appearance — for us to physically touch Him today.

But I have good news for you: While His physical body is in heaven, He has another Body here on earth.

> **Romans 12:4-5 —** For just as each of us has one body with many members, and these members do not all have the same function, so in Christ we, though many, form one body, and each member belongs to all the others.

> **1 Corinthians 12:27** — Now you are the body of Christ, and each one of you is a part of it.
>
> **Ephesians 4:15-16** — Instead, speaking the truth in love, we will grow to become in every respect the mature body of him who is the head, that is, Christ. From him the whole body, joined and held together by every supporting ligament, grows and builds itself up in love, as each part does its work.

Something we don't often realize is that in that quarter of cases where Jesus said, "Your faith has healed you," He wasn't talking about the person's perfect faith in God. If that were the case, then the person could have been healed without coming to Jesus. Remember, most people didn't realize Jesus was God-in-the-flesh while He walked among us. To them He was often seen as little more than a teacher or prophet who consistently ministered healing.

So whenever Jesus praised someone for their faith, it was actually their faith in Him as a minister to consistently supply healing on behalf of the Father. Again, if it was their faith in God, then they wouldn't have needed Jesus (who, in their eyes, was at most the Messiah but still a mere man).

I don't know a single sick Christian who doesn't have faith that if they physically touched Jesus, they'd be healed. The problem is that we don't have that faith in each other as the Body of Christ. We don't actually believe that "if I touch you, I'm going to touch Jesus." We're not convinced that the person in front of us can deliver.

We might say that's not true, but why, then, do we hunt down faith-healers and people with big ministries and lots of testimonies? Why to we chase them like celebrities and try to receive prayer from them? On the surface, it's because we see their results and believe that they can help us too. But beneath the surface, it's because we're more enamored with them than we are with the Body of Jesus. We don't believe the socially-awkward guy in our church who got saved a couple weeks ago has anything to offer. We don't believe that the four-year-old in the nursery who loves Jesus has anything to offer. We don't believe that the sweet old lady with the walker and too much perfume has anything to offer. We don't even think our pastor has anything to offer! We're looking for Jesus everywhere else than our own home church. We don't actually believe that the Christians around us are the Body of Christ.

But where does James say to go?

> **James 5:14-15** — Is anyone among you sick? Let them call the elders [mature Christians] of the church to pray over them and anoint them with oil in the name of the Lord. And the prayer offered in faith will make the sick person well; the Lord will raise them up.

> If they have sinned, they will be
> forgiven. (clarification added)

Jesus said that signs like "healing the sick" would be found among "those who believe" (Mark 16:17-18). He said, "Very truly I tell you, whoever believes in me will do the works I have been doing, and they will do even greater things than these, because I am going to the Father" (John 14:12). Healing is a ministry of EVERY Christian. (As a side note, I believe the only reason James specified "elders" is because he knew that those who have a mature walk with the Lord are more likely to contend for healing without giving up or compromising their theology to explain away a lack of results. And the reason he sends us to our own local church is because these are the people who know us and care enough about us to persevere until we're whole.)

A misunderstanding of healing ministry has led us into a subtle form of idolatry as we look for special faith-healers to fix us in the place of Jesus. We look for famous ministers from somewhere else rather than obeying the biblical mandate to simply touch the Body of Christ, which He has placed locally and within our reach.

Biblically speaking, the only prescription for a sick Christian is to have local mature believers minister to him or her. You don't need to have perfect faith. You don't have to eliminate all doubt. You don't have to confess the right promises or quote the right scriptures. You don't have to uncover secret sins or figure out spiritual roots. You don't have to hunt down a faith-healer. You don't have to perform. And you certainly don't have to figure out how to minister to yourself (although there's nothing wrong with trying). All these things are nice if they happen, but none of them are Biblical responsibilities of a sick person.

The only thing you need to do is touch Jesus, and He's right there in the nearest Christian.

If you need healing right now, I want you to find the nearest Christian and simply touch even the edge of their clothing. Maybe even just their shadow (Acts 5:15). Or perhaps even just something they have touched (Acts 19:11-12). Recognize that he or she is a part of Jesus' body, and expect that when you touch that person, you are touching Jesus Himself.

Then immediately test out your condition. Try to do something you couldn't do. If you're healed, I want to hear a testimony, so please comment below!

But if — like me — you're not yet healed, then I want you to keep seeking out ministry from those around you. You don't need to chase down a big-name minister. All you need is the Body of Christ, and that can be found in nearly every city in America and also all over the world. Keep reaching out to other Christians in faith, knowing that they are physical extensions of Jesus standing right in front of you. Let people pray for you and even ask them to command your sickness to leave in the name of Jesus.

Christians are always growing. And that's great news because it means every time someone ministers to you in Jesus' name, they're more like Jesus than they were last time; and that makes the healing more likely to happen! The process of experiencing healing is just as much about our own perseverance as it is about the continual growth of the Church as we are all conformed to "the whole measure of the fullness of Christ." We're not fully there yet, but we're on our way, and more people are being healed every single day.

I'm believing with you that you and I will *both* be healed in no time at all.

Never give up.

Be blessed!
--Art

NOTE: One month later, after ministry from "ordinary believers," I was completely healed of Crohn's Disease.

Appendix B:

TESTIMONIES OF VICTORY

I thought it might be encouraging to find some testimonies from people who have been in your shoes as a family member of a sick loved one and have seen a breakthrough. Whenever you're feeling discouraged or tired of contending for a miracle, try reading some of these stories to build up your faith and encourage you to expect a miracle.

SHANNAN HOWLETT — DETROIT, TEXAS

WHEN MY DAUGHTER, ABIGAIL, WAS ONLY TWO months old, I began to notice little red dots all over her body. I really became alarmed when I saw unexplained bruises on her and blood in her stools.

We immediately scheduled an appointment with her pediatrician. Since her doctor had specialized in hematology in medical school, he was able to diagnose the problem right away. He thought she had a blood disease called Idiopathic Thrombocytopenic Purpura (ITP). He referred us to a children's hospital, and we were scheduled to see a specialist the following day.

Upon arrival they ran a battery of tests, which included a spinal tap. This poor baby girl was taken from me kicking and screaming. They rolled her into a ball and extracted marrow from her spine—and all this without any anesthesia (they said she was too young to be anesthetized). My husband and I were also tested to see if this could be hereditary. All the tests confirmed our pediatrician's diagnosis.

ITP is an incurable disease of the blood. It is characterized by a low platelet count and a propensity to bleed. Doctors don't know what causes it, and there is very little that can be done to treat it. My daughter's platelet count was extremely low at 14,000 per cu/ml. A normal platelet count is between 150,000-400,000 per cu/ml.

They said Abigail was the youngest person they had ever seen with this disease, and so they hesitated to give her any medications or treatments that might interfere with her growth and development. They'd had some success with steroid treatments boosting the platelet count, but because this treatment could cause cerebral hemorrhaging, they would only use this on her as an emergency and last resort if her platelet count fell below 10,000. They also cautioned us about being in any type of accident that might cause internal bleeding. Platelets play a crucial part in the blood clotting process by forming a platelet plug; otherwise, you might bleed to death. They indicated that in a life-threatening situation they might not be able to get her bleeding under control, which could be fatal.

Our life settled into a series of doctor visits—weekly at first and then every two weeks. She would have the heel of her foot pricked to extract enough blood to get a platelet count.

Over time, Abigail became terrified of anyone in a white coat. Regardless of where we were, she would immediately begin crying and become very clingy anytime she spotted someone in a white coat.

This was very traumatic for a new mom and dad. *Wasn't this supposed to be a time filled with joy? Didn't God speak to me that I was going to have a little girl and to name her Abigail? Surely He wasn't going to let her die.* I didn't understand why all this was happening.

During this time I prayed and sought God a lot. One day I distinctly heard the Lord speak, "She will be well." I would hold onto these four little words over the next few months with my whole being. This would be the only thing I ever heard the Lord speak concerning this situation, but it was all I needed. I now had His promise.

As the months passed, Abigail became increasingly more active. One day as she was learning to crawl, she fell, landing on her lip, which started to bleed. I couldn't get it to stop. I remember praying and asking God to stop the bleeding. It eventually did stop, but I was left with a terrible sinking feeling: *How would I be able to manage an active child and the normal bruises and scrapes of life?*

An older child's actions can somewhat be controlled, but not a baby's.

When Abigail was nine months old, I took her to the doctor for her usual blood test and received some distressing news. Apparently, for the last two months her white blood count had been abnormal and she would have to go back to the children's hospital for another round of tests, including a spinal tap. She was scheduled for admission into the hospital on Friday (three days away).

This news was almost more than I could bear. It seemed like my whole world was spiraling down around me. The previous Sunday I heard a song— "The Captain of the Host"—at church, and I could not get this tune out of my head. The words go like this:

> *The Captain of the Host is Jesus.*
> *We are following in His footsteps.*
> *No foe can stand against us in the fray.*

This became my battle mantra. I began to sing it night and day.

Sometime between Tuesday and Friday, I became desperate. God had made a promise (His revealed will about my situation) to me months before. I had to "touch the hem of His garment." We seldom went to church on Wednesday nights, but desperate times call for desperate measures. We were the first in line when asked if anyone needed prayer for healing. Abigail had been prayed for hundreds of times before, but that wasn't going to stop me now.

A young woman spoke a simple prayer over her: "Be healed in Jesus' name."

On Friday I took Abigail to the hospital. During her tests, I was sitting in the waiting room hearing conversations about very sick little children who were suffering or who had died. It could have been very depressing, but the "Captain of the Host" was roaring though my mind.

After what seemed like an eternity, our doctor came waltzing into the room, and he was literally scratching his head. He asked me if I had given my blood that day. I told him no. He said, "It's a funny thing, Abigail's platelet count was over 300,000 per cu/ml with a normal white count, and I was sure it had to be a mistake. I was wondering if maybe your blood had been tested instead of hers?"

I was speechless. The God of the universe had healed my child. I just wanted to fall to my knees and worship Him.

Since Abigail was the youngest patient with ITP they had ever seen, the doctor would not release her until she had been monitored for a year. Every month I would take her for her blood test, and the results would proclaim, "Our God heals!" Halleluiah!

Abigail is now thirty years old.

CLAYTON COOTS — FORT PAYNE, ALABAMA

AROUND JUNE OF 2016, I WAS LEAVING MY LOCAL Walmart and ran into my Uncle Virgil. He told me my Aunt Kathy was at home, about 20 minutes away. She had been laid up in bed for two weeks with two slipped discs and damage to one of her sciatic nerves. The pain had been affecting her for a couple of months.

As I left Walmart, I immediately tried calling Aunt Kathy several times. I knew God wanted to heal her, but no one picked up the phone.

The following week, I was off work. I called her home again, and one of my other aunts (Yvonne) answered the phone. I learned that Aunt Kathy was still in bed and in chronic pain. I asked if I could come out and lay hands on her for healing. Aunt Yvonne invited me to come on over.

When I arrived, there were several other family members in the living room. I went back to the bedroom where Aunt Kathy and Aunt Yvonne were. Aunt Kathy was laying flat of her back. She was in so much pain she literally had tears running down her cheeks.

I began to question her about her pain level on a scale of 1 to 10. I wanted to have a way to assess whether anything was changing as we ministered.

She said the pain was over 10.

I put my hand on her side, close to her lower back, and began to thank the Lord for her and for His love for her. I thanked God for not wanting her to suffer like this. And I thanked the Lord for what I knew He was fixing to do.

I then commanded the discs, nerves, muscles, vertebra and sciatic nerve to be healed and to come back into alignment in Jesus' name. I told the pain to "leave her body right now in Jesus' name." I only held my hand there for about 10 or 15 seconds to allow the Holy Spirit to do His healing work on her back.

I then asked her again what her pain level was.

She reported that it had dropped to about a 6.

I laid my hand back on her side again, thanked the Father for bringing it down to a 6, and then began commanding the back to be completely healed and all pain to go in Jesus' name.

I asked her again about her pain level, and it had dropped to about a 2.

I could see a sense of relief on her face. She felt so much better that she asked me and my Aunt Yvonne to prop her up in the bed with a couple pillows behind her back.

We were all thanking the Lord and praising Him for a few minutes. Then Aunt Yvonne went to the kitchen to make a pot of coffee.

After 1 or 2 minutes I walked to the kitchen as well. Once there, though, I realized I had left my drink in the bedroom. So I walked back down the hall, and as I entered the bedroom, my Aunt Kathy was already out of the bed and had her house coat on with a big smile on her face.

She went to the kitchen, sat at the table, and drank coffee with us. She told us that all the pain was gone. We sat and talked about our beloved Savior Jesus for a while before I left.

About two weeks later, my Aunt Kathy and Aunt Yvonne went on vacation to the beach. To this day, she has had no more problems with her back.

Some people go into situations like this expecting that they'll have to persevere. To use the word "persevere" sounds like having faith that God will heal someone later or "in God's own time." In the Bible, Jesus and His disciples never prayed for days or months. The healings took place either immediately, within the hour, or as they walked away. Be encouraged by that example and expect the same thing whenever you minister to anyone. Jesus wants to do the same through you. old.

JESSICA BLOOD – WOODWORTH, LOUISIANA

WHEN MY DAUGHTER, EDEN, WAS BORN, SHE HAD a benign lipoma (lump) on her forehead right at the hair line. The doctors we were seeing at the time had no idea what it was, so we were referred to a neurologist.

After several days of testing and MRIs, the diagnosis was that the lipoma we could see on the outside was an outward view of the one inside of her brain. She was missing her *corpus callosum*—the center part of her brain, which would allow the right side of her brain to communicate with the left side. We were told that our daughter would be mentally handicapped and that we should never expect her to be on the same level socially or mentally as other children her age.

I had only been following Jesus for six months. I had a nominal Catholic background and had never prayed anything except the typical Catholic prayers. But my friend had given me a Bible that had study notes in the back. When we came home from that appointment, the Lord directed me to a section of notes in my Bible that discussed praying for a miracle. It instructed me to simply speak it out and believe it. At the time I thought that had to be too easy, but not really knowing any better, I did as instructed. I truly believed that the miracle happened right then and there simply because I knew I believed.

I prayed that day and everyday afterward. Nothing seemed to be changing on the outside, but I knew in my heart that God was working.

Five months later, we arrived for the surgery that could last anywhere from 10 to 35 hours. An entire team of doctors and specialists would perform multiple surgeries, and the brain surgeon would be opening up our ten-month-old baby's skull to perform brain surgery.

After only one hour, the first doctor came out to report that the surgery was finished. He said that what they found was nothing more than an enlarged vein—not the serious problems shown in the MRIs and other tests. The doctors saw what I already knew in my heart was true. We arrived home from surgery just 6 hours after completion.

Our daughter, Eden, is perfect. She is currently fourteen-years-old in the ninth grade and has never had any issues mentally or socially. The Lord formed what was not there and miraculously healed her. He is the Healer. He is our Comfort in times of uncertainty.

JONATHAN BRENNEMAN – RIO DE JANEIRO, BRAZIL

MY SISTER WAS FARSIGHTED. I HAD LAID HANDS on her and commanded her eyes to focus several times but without seeing any results. I wanted to see her healed, and I wasn't going to stop just because I hadn't seen it yet. I simply figured, *I'm growing in faith and in Jesus.*

Some people thought I was presumptuous to act as if I could know God's will—that He wanted my sister to be healed. They would tell me to "seek God's face, not His hand."

One day, my brother and I prayed for a blind

lady. She said she felt God's power, and while her eyes didn't fully open right then, she said she had slight improvement. The next day, we told my sister about our experience praying for the blind lady. Suddenly, my sister felt something moving in her eyes.

That weekend she went to her eye doctor, and he told her she didn't need glasses anymore.

If you are believing for a family member's healing, just keep moving forward and focusing on what God is doing. Continue ministering to people outside of your family, and don't think of your family member's case as any different. Keep sharing testimonies, and go for it again and again if need be. Stand firm. uncertainty.

RACHEL SHOCKLEY — SPRINGFIELD, MISSOURI

THE DAY BEFORE THANKSGIVING 2005, MY boyfriend, Tom, was in a car wreck. He had a Traumatic Brain Injury (TBI), a broken collarbone, broken ribs, internal bleeding, and a broken neck at C6 and C7. They put him on a ventilator and said that if he survived forty-eight hours, he would live but would never walk again.

Some didn't believe he would ever regain his cognitive function after the TBI and wanted me to end the relationship. Even Tom's mother advised me to break up with him due to his crippled condition.

169

Tom and I were students at Central Bible College. Our campus pastor went to see him and said that without a miracle, Tom would die. He didn't seem to expect one, though. He said, "I will believe with you, but I'm here for you if God says 'no' to healing."

I thought, *How can this even be happening? I can't marry this man if he's dead!* I felt confusion, shock, and desperation. But I wasn't willing to give up on him.

Almost all of our fellow students from CBC were back at home with their families for the Thanksgiving weekend, so when I called my roommate to tell her what happened to Tom, she called our other friends for me. They all put Tom on the "prayer chains" at their various churches. We had people literally all over the world praying for Tom.

After only two days, Tom was off the ventilator. When Tom woke up, he didn't know who I was. When they moved him to a regular hospital room, he had a Christian nurse who found out he was in Bible college and started quoting scriptures to him. Tom would quote verses back each time. He didn't know who I was or who some of his other family members were, but he could still quote Scripture!

Within one week, he was released from the hospital and transferred to a rehab hospital. The doctor at the rehab hospital told Tom that he didn't think he would ever walk again. But Tom fired back, "I will walk again because I serve a big God."

I continued to visit him every couple of days

for the next couple weeks. The Monday I went to see him, he was in a wheelchair. When I arrived two days later on Wednesday, Tom walked right up to me and gave me a hug. In the beginning, the doctors told us he would be in the hospital or rehab until March 2006, but in another two weeks, Tom was released from rehab and even started the Spring semester at CBC that January—only six weeks after the wreck.

About a year later, in February of 2007, Tom and I were married.

Sometimes miracles are instantaneous. Other times we persevere. God knows your heart and understands when you're upset and scared, but keep the faith. Trust God's goodness, and never give up on loving Him no matter what happens.

MELISSA GLORIOSO – TORRANCE, CALIFORNIA

ON JANUARY 2, 2012, MY HUSBAND, TONY, WAS feeling a little off and drove 22 miles on the freeway in the wrong direction before he realized something was wrong. He couldn't figure out how to get back to where he was supposed to be, so he called me. I didn't think anything was really wrong (except that he's not very good with directions!), and I was busy in a big meeting 2 hours away with the managerial department of a hospital. I told him that he needed to find a gas station and ask for help.

He called 2 more times, concerned and

confused, but I assured him that I didn't know how to help him—other than to tell him that he really needed to find that gas station. Again, I didn't think too much of it and returned to the business at hand.

That night at home, he told me that he was battling something and asked me to pray for him. He had put on a sweatshirt and a blanket, which was quite odd since he usually only wears sleeveless shirts and never gets cold. So I prayed, and we went to bed.

In the middle of the night, I heard a loud crash and called out to Tony (since I had noticed that he was not in bed), asking him if he knew what the noise was. He replied from the bathroom that he didn't know, so I figured I'd better get up to investigate.

I first looked around the bedroom and didn't see anything. When I came to the bathroom, I found him lying on the floor. I asked if he was OK, and he replied, "Yes, I'm fine."

He laid there on his side, but his head wasn't on the floor like most people's would be. His neck was straight, in line with his spine, which I found quite odd.

As I spoke with him, I could tell that he didn't even realize he was lying on the floor. I thought hard about what I should do, trying to remember my medical training. I figured after a couple of minutes his blood should start flowing normally and he should be able to sit up. So after a couple of minutes I asked, "Why don't you sit up and see how you feel?"

He sat up with his back on the door jam and talked to me a little more, and then his eyes rolled upwards and his head fell fast onto his chest.

My first thought was, *NO! This is not going to happen like this!*

I started commanding him to wake up as I spun him around and laid him flat down on the floor. He opened his eyes one more time, looked around, and then his eyes rolled back into his head as he breathed out one long breath.

That was it.

I started saying in a demanding voice, "TONY, IN JESUS' NAME, WAKE UP!" I repeated this over and over for what seemed like forever. During this time, I felt compelled to give him 2 chest compressions and only 2. I also slapped his face a few times (as seen on TV!) and kept shouting loudly and forcefully, "TONY, IN JESUS' NAME, WAKE UP!"

At one point I could hear a voice in my head saying, "You'd better call 911..." But I couldn't leave him like that. I knew in my spirit that this was a spiritual attack, and they wouldn't be able to do anything for him anyway.

After quite some time, Tony suddenly opened his eyes and exclaimed, "Boy! I feel better than I have felt all week!"

All I could say (repeatedly) was, "Thank You, Jesus! Thank You, Jesus! Thank You, Jesus!"

Tony laid there for a few more minutes and then stood up, looked at himself in the mirror and said, "Wow, I'm white."

I said, "I know. I think you'd better go lay down."

We went back to bed, prayed a little, and went to sleep. I slept with my head near his head and my hand on his heart (just to make sure the devil wasn't going to try anymore tricky business).

As the next day progressed, Tony's voice grew stronger and stronger. A couple of days later he told me that he felt 100% back to normal.

For quite a few days I couldn't stop looking at him and smiling. He kept asking what I was smiling at. I told him, "I like you much better talking and pink."

Tony told me that while he was dead, he was talking to someone. When he heard me yelling, he told the person to whom he was talking, "That's my wife, I better go see what she wants." And that's when he woke up.

What Satan meant for evil has only strengthened our faith, and our marriage. This test turned into a testimony that encourages us and many others.

LYNETTE GINGRICH — FREEBURG, PENNSYLVANIA

IN 1988, WHEN MY HUSBAND, TIM, WAS TWENTY-one-years-old, he was working on a dry kiln roof, about 30 to 35 feet up and hit a 12,000 volt power line, which blew him off the building. He fell to the ground, resulting in a fractured skull, broken neck, broken back, ruptured spleen, and an amputated toe on his right foot. He was paralyzed from the chest down with what doctors said was a severed spinal cord. They removed his spleen and took out a lot of muscle from his right leg due to electrical burns.

The first week was very hard. We had only been married about two years. We had two small children, ages two and one. First they weren't sure if my husband would live. Later they said he would never leave a wheelchair. I determined in my heart that I would stand by Tim's side through it all and would not give up.

I lost fifteen pounds in three days. I would come home to see my children and then drive back to the hospital a few hours later. My heart would race as I approached the hospital because every day the reports were worse than the day before.

Tim and I chose to believe God for a miracle. Many people simply didn't understand that God still heals today. Some even tried to convince us that Tim's condition was somehow God's will. But we continued to believe God wanted something better.

Little by little we witnessed the Father's faithfulness. A week into the ordeal, we moved hospitals, and new tests showed new results. Three weeks later, bone fragments that were visible in previous x-rays had miraculously disappeared (as shown by new x-rays) so that no additional surgeries were needed.

About three months after the accident, before Tim went to sleep, Father God reminded him of all the prayers and the miracles he had seen. God reminded him of Philippians 4:6 and how to give thanks while making your requests. Tim started to give thanks for what God had already done and then fell asleep.

A few hours later, Tim woke up and started moving his legs for the first time in three months. Today, he can walk unaided. Many more miracles have happened too, including no more complications from the missing spleen. And the miracles continue to happen today.

If you're seeking a miracle for a family member, it's best if you can find a group of people who are strong in faith and believe God is able and willing to heal. Keep connected with them, and dismiss the negative and discouraging words of others. Surround yourself with a community of believers who can help you when you feel down and will continue to speak words of life and faith over you and your loved one.

**NOTE: You can see Tim Gingrich sharing his testimony and standing in the movie *Paid in Full*. More information is available on the "Additional Resources" page at the end of this book.

ABOUT THE AUTHOR

Art Thomas is a missionary-evangelist who travels the world to preach the Gospel, plant churches, train pastors, and equip Christians to live like Jesus. He has trained tens of thousands of people to minister healing in Jesus' name through church meetings, books, articles, YouTube videos, and the movie he co-directed and produced, *Paid in Full – God's Desire to Heal through Today's Believers.*

Art has been miraculously healed of multiple incurable conditions including a heart murmur, scars on his face from second-degree burns, chronic sinus infections, seasonal allergies, ADHD, degenerative disc disease, and Crohn's Disease. His years of suffering and contending for miracles give him a unique perspective on healing ministry that has been a great encouragement to many.

Art is the President and CEO of *Wildfire Ministries International* and lives with his wife Robin and their two boys, Josiah and Jeremiah, in Plymouth, Michigan.

ADDITIONAL RESOURCES:

For learning to minister healing:

➤ *Paid in Full* (DVD movie)

➤ *Paid in Full 40-Day Healing Ministry Activation Manual* (book)

➤ *Paid in Full* 8-Week Small Group DVD and Curriculum (DVD and PDF download)

For studying God's Will to Heal:

➤ *Spiritual Tweezers – Removing Paul's Thorn in the Flesh and Other False Objections to God's Will for Healing* (book)

For renewing your mind and building hope:

➤ *Limitless Hope – Renewing Your Mind for Supernatural Living* (book)

All materials are available at www.SupernaturalTruth.com

There are also plenty of **free videos, articles, and audio sermons** under the "Free Media" tab at www.SupernaturalTruth.com.

Please consider sharing this book with a friend and writing a review on Amazon.com.

Additional copies available at
www.SupernaturalTruth.com